ADAM REECE, DPT, OCS

Survive and Thrive

Mastering Orthopedic Physical Therapy in a High Volume Clinic

Copyright © 2024 by Adam Reece, DPT, OCS

All rights reserved. No part of this publication may be reproduced, stored or transmitted in any form or by any means, electronic, mechanical, photocopying, recording, scanning, or otherwise without written permission from the publisher. It is illegal to copy this book, post it to a website, or distribute it by any other means without permission.

Adam Reece, DPT, OCS has no responsibility for the persistence or accuracy of URLs for external or third-party Internet Websites referred to in this publication and does not guarantee that any content on such Websites is, or will remain, accurate or appropriate.

Designations used by companies to distinguish their products are often claimed as trademarks. All brand names and product names used in this book and on its cover are trade names, service marks, trademarks and registered trademarks of their respective owners. The publishers and the book are not associated with any product or vendor mentioned in this book. None of the companies referenced within the book have endorsed the book.

First edition

This book was professionally typeset on Reedsy. Find out more at reedsy.com

Contents

Preface	v
1 Welcome to the Clinic	1
Embracing the Learning Curve	1
Trial and Error	2
Navigating the Clinic Environment	4
Overwhelming Moments	8
2 Building Strong Foundations	11
Patient-Centered Care	11
Empathy Goes a Long Way	14
Establishing Trust and Rapport	19
Effective Communication Skills	20
3 Time Management	22
Scheduling Strategies: The Calendar Conundrum	22
Documenting Efficiently: The Paperwork Marathon	27
Prioritizing Patient Care: The Urgency Dilemma	29
4 Clinical Skills for Success	33
Assessing Orthopedic Conditions	33
Creating Effective Treatment Plans	38
Manual Therapy Techniques	44
Keeping an Eye on Discharge	46
5 Collaborative Care	48
Inter-professional Relationships	48
Effective Communication with Physicians	50
Consultations and Referrals	51

Teamwork in Patient Care	52
6　Work Life Balance	56
Stress Management Strategies	56
Preventing Burnout	57
Self-Care for PTs	60
Finding Work-Life Balance	63
7　Patient Education & Empowerment	66
Educating Patients About Their Conditions	66
Setting Realistic Expectations to Improve Outcomes	68
Promoting Compliance	70
Empowering Patients for Long-Term Health	71
8　Lifelong Learning	73
Staying Current with Evidence-Based Practice	73
The Importance of Mentors	76
Pursuing Specializations and Certifications	78
Charting Your Career Path	79
9　Celebrate Your Successes	83
Recognizing Milestones	83
Positive affirmations	86
Celebrate the Small Wins	87
Seeking Feedback and Improvement	88
Inspiring Future Graduates	91
10　APPENDIX	96
Empathy Statements	98
Smart phrases	101
Daily Checklist for Managing the Urgency Dilemma	108
Clinical Assessment Clusters for Common Orthopedic Conditions	111
Recommended Reading	129
Certifications / Specializations	133
Templates for Clinical Mentorship	137

Preface

Welcome to Outpatient Orthopedic Physical Therapy – it's head spinning, it's chaotic and some days the caseload can feel like you are drinking from a fire hydrant. Here, real-time chaos, progress, and surprises are daily norms, testing your knowledge, patience, and dedication to helping patients regain mobility and independence. In the clinic fray, you are expected to manage a rotating door of patients, endless paperwork, and collateral responsibilities on a daily basis with effectiveness and efficiency.

Clinic days are packed with patient assessments, individualized treatment plans, and multitasking across various roles, all while maintaining professionalism and empathy. The electronic medical records (EMR) system becomes your indispensable tool for managing this constant flow of information and tasks while simultaneously serving as the bane of your existence.

This book isn't about dry theories; it's an unofficial guide filled with real-world insights, practical advice, and humor to help you excel in your orthopedic PT career. This book focuses on patient-centered care, emphasizing the importance of treating individuals, not just conditions. You'll learn time management, effective treatment planning, and the essentials of healthcare teamwork. We'll also address handling stress, avoiding burnout, and maintaining work-life balance.

Here, you'll find strategies for educating and empowering patients, insights into evidence-based practice, and tips for networking and career development. This guide celebrates your achievements, encourages continuous learning, and inspires you to be a role model for future PT graduates.

Your journey in the unpredictable yet rewarding world of outpatient orthopedic physical therapy starts now. Embrace this adventure of challenges, successes, and impactful experiences. So, let's head into the clinic and start on your journey of growth, learning, and making a difference, aka giving a damn.

1

Welcome to the Clinic

Embracing the Learning Curve

Get ready for a crash course in what it means to truly embrace the learning curve. You might have aced your PT program, but the clinic is a whole different beast, and it's about to throw you some curve balls.

I have worked in outpatient orthopedics for 10 years as of writing this book. However, the first 6 years were spent in one-on-one clinics. It was in 2020, that I took a staff Physical Therapy position with a truly high-volume clinic. I had historically treated one patient at a time for 45-60 minutes. However, I wanted to move my work closer to home, so I joined a clinic where I was expected to see anywhere between 16-24 patient's a day, 5 days a week. I lasted a measly three months and turned my notice over to the director. The clinic had a great team of clinicians and administrators that encouraged me to stay. I reduced my hours to 32, only worked 4 days a week and began an in-depth process of professional growth and development that resulted in me creating a systematic approach to not just survive but thrive in a high-volume clinical setting. I have since treated upwards of 27 patient's in one day. It wasn't pretty and I don't recommend this style of clinical practice but it can be done. Without a systematic process of evaluations and treatments, there was no way I would have been able to handle that kind of load. With insurance companies reimbursing less for Physical Therapy services while cost of living, education and real estate escalate; there will be a need to increase the volume of patients treated per provider during the day to make up for clinic overhead. As the saying goes, "It is what it is". You will enjoy a long prosperous career if you prepare your mind for the cacophony of ringing phones, the pulling from patients in the clinic, and the constant paperwork that is the outpatient orthopedic clinic.

Trial and Error

In a PT classroom, everything feels systematic and predictable. PT's learn the theories, study the anatomy, and practice the techniques, and the solutions to patient problems/case scenarios. But in the clinic, it's different. Patients rarely present as textbook cases, and their responses to treatments often vary because outcomes are intertwined with socioeconomic, emotional and social beliefs and perceptions. It is a world where X-rays and MRIs don't always provide the full picture, where patients' health perceptions seem disconnected from their physical conditions, and where progress is often more of a zigzag than a straight line. It is a place where the ideal treatment plan on paper might not yield the expected results in reality.

I encourage you to embrace trial and error as a guiding principle, a mantra that "it is okay not to have all the answers upfront". Understand that each patient is a unique puzzle, and the key to solving it often involves trying different approaches, adjusting treatments on the fly, and closely observing how the patient responded. Some exercises that seem perfect in theory might not work for a particular individual, and others that seemed unconventional could yield remarkable results. Reframe how you view a high-volume clinic. Instead of only seeing chaos, see instead a dynamic environment that will constantly refine your skills, hone your intuition, and help you discover the art of tailoring treatments to individual needs. Take the approach that mistakes aren't failures but stepping stones to progress. When an exercise or treatment doesn't produce the expected outcome, it's not a setback; it's an opportunity to learn, adjust, and find a better way. I recommend you keep a journal of your daily treatments to help you think about the way you think, this is called metacognition. In the appendix, you will find an example of daily journaling to help facilitate growth. If this interests you, find a link to my book "Mindful Practice: A Metacognition Journal for Physical Therapists" at www.deltaperformancerehab.com. The book includes daily entry pages, prompts for deeper reflection, goal setting, monthly reflection pages, a progress tracker, tips for continuous improvement, and recommendations on additional resources.

Navigating the Clinic Environment

You'll quickly realize that time management isn't just a skill; it's a survival tool. Balancing patient care, paperwork, and squeezing in a bathroom break requires ninja-level scheduling skills. Expect a few hiccups along the way. You can't do it all at once. Start each day by identifying your top priorities. Make notes on your schedule that capture the first few minutes of a patient's treatment for that day (i.e. MHP for pain, recumbent bike x 6' then Dynamic Warm-up, etc.) or notes about paperwork (i.e. PN, D/C) and include the outcome tool they need, then pass that information along to your tech's or front office. Some tasks can wait; others can't. Divide your day into blocks. Dedicate specific blocks to patient treatments, paperwork, phone calls, and even breaks. Stick to these blocks as closely as possible to maintain a sense of structure. You're not a one-person show. Learn to delegate tasks when possible. I have an incredible team of support staff that assist me with paperwork, scheduling, and basic exercises, allowing me to focus on skilled patient care. I perform targeted manual therapy focusing on regenerative strategies like ASTYM, improve tissue extensibility with cupping trigger point release (maybe dry needling if approved in your state), and then joint mobilizations/manipulations to improve functional mobility for the treatment and then move onto patient and injury appropriate functional exercises. Spending time with patients on a plinth is not time efficient. I fully support manual therapy, but I also fully support patient independence. Helping the patient be more independent frees your time to work with other patients, take a phone call, write a letter to a referring provider as well as improves their ultimate outcomes. With regard to manual therapy, get in and get out and move on to more functional and integrative exercises.

EMR can be a blessing and a curse. Utilize shortcuts, templates, and voice-to-text tools to speed up documentation without sacrificing quality. Remember, concise notes are often more valuable than lengthy ones. Through experience, I have determined I am absolutely terrible with voice-to-text applications. I rely heavily on smart phrases that I have accumulated over the years. These smart phrases do not provide any specifics, they simply serve as information for future reference. Examples include:

"Patient tolerated the last visit well without increased or with increased symptoms later that day/overnight/the next day. Pt is performing their HEP as instructed / not as instructed due to _____ without increased symptoms or difficulty or with increased symptoms or difficulty due to _____."

Then I include any specific information that is relevant to the patient's case, i.e. upcoming provider visits, imaging studies, or procedures. Every provider has their own voice when it comes to documentation, find yours and then spend time upfront (maybe even off hours) making smart phrases, it will save you time in the future. I share a free copy of smart phrases in the appendix to get you started.

When it comes to evaluations, assess patients thoroughly but efficiently. Don't spend so much time assessing everything you can. Clear red flags then move on to meat and potatoes. Don't check reflexes if paresthesias aren't present in the subjective. Don't check an anterior draw if the mechanism of injury is over use. Find a consistent systematic method of assessment and perform it on everyone! The more you practice it, the faster you will be without missing important information. I use the Selective Functional Movement Assessment. I find it helps get me focused on the most important aspects of the patient's chief complaint. I can then breakout other areas at future visits to explore regional interdependence. That's my system, I highly recommend the SFMA but ultimately you be you. Take courses from the Gray Institute, Postural Restoration Institute, whatever floats your boat but master them with consistent practice.

I also make sure to speak with patient's upfront about treatment times and introduce them to my support staff on day one to ensure they understand how the clinic flows. The plan of care should be fairly well laid out after the first or second visit. I have created a template of treatments for common Physical Therapy referrals that I utilize to help guide my plan of care and exercise flow sheet prior to the patient's first follow-up visit. Every patient is unique, so I don't have any expectation that my template will fit exactly but it's a good place to start. I hope you consider this approach b/c chances are you will be super busy when the patient comes back for their first follow-up visit and your head will be reeling simply trying to remember who the heck they are and why they're in the clinic. You may even ask yourself, "Did I do their eval?", even though it was two days ago. If you automate your flow sheet for "what happens at their next visit" while you complete their eval note, you will look like someone who has their head on tight. If you don't, you look lost in the weeds. You will find more about templates in Chapter 4.

This affords me the opportunity to document quickly and engage with the patient without looking unprepared. This method also ensures my support staff or the PTA have an understanding of what the patient is working on if they touch the patient at future follow up visits. At my clinic, the PT's/PTA's set aside an extended lunch about once a quarter to sound board off one another regarding examination/testing methods, manual therapy techniques, exercises, semantics, plan of care design and space utilization. This makes sure we are all on the same page and maintains continuity of care between providers (aka, communication).

It's hard to be time efficient if your workspace and clinic is that of my kids' playroom. You and your support staff need to keep your treatment area and desk organized. Every tool, folder, document has a place and stay consistent with putting them there at all times to avoid wasting precious minutes searching. Be retentive with organization. I have spent way too much time tracking down goniometers, squat wedges, and BOSU's in my past. These days, my problem is setting up for patients ahead of time and my support staff puts my stuff away before my patient has a chance to use the equipment. This is simply a problem with my communication to my support staff and requires me to take a few extra seconds to bring my staff into the fold on what I'm doing with the equipment. This is what I call "a good problem to have".

As Physical Therapists, we wear the catchall badge of honor being the professionals to whom providers from many disciplines refer their patients. I would wager that most of you reading this are Physical Therapists who genuinely want to help everyone, but recognize your limits. I work at a sports Physical Therapy clinic that is affiliated with local high schools, community colleges, and semi-pro and professional athletics. However, we still see a large patient population with non-sport related injuries, those who are Medicare beneficiaries, injured in an MVA or on the job. We see patients with neurologic impairments and fall risks but there comes a point when, based on the nature of a busy clinic, that you must politely decline additional tasks or appointments if the clinic setting jeopardizes your ability to provide quality care to existing patients. As an example, I worked with a patient referred to PT for dystonia. Her referring provider loved our approach to patients with Parkinson's Disease and she felt this patient with dystonia should see us. However, the patient's symptoms became quite reactive to the clinic volume and noise. She became emotionally labile and we had to find her a more suitable clinic. Basic wheelchair assessment, no problem in my clinic but I don't have time to perform in-depth power chair assessments. The front office staff and PT providers in my clinic have discussed strengths and weaknesses to help determine what condition or impairment is appropriate for our clinic and who may be better suited with treatment at a different clinic that is appropriate for the patient. Of course, keeping patient's in house is important for business but this should be balanced with patient outcomes and safety. If you have another clinic or sister-clinic that would be a better fit, that would be a great option, business stays in-house sort of speak or at least stays within your network.

Overwhelming Moments

Let me highlight one more time... high-volume is going to be the norm. There are days when you'll feel like you're drowning in a sea of patient charts, phone calls, audits, physician letters/thank you notes, and emails waiting in your inbox for reply. It happens to the best of us, and when it does, it can be downright overwhelming. I was overwhelmed, I even put in my notice only after a couple months of working in my first high-volume clinic. However, I found a way to make it work and so will you.

When you're overwhelmed, the first step is to take a deep breath. Seriously, just stop and breathe for a moment. It might sound simple, but it can do wonders for your clarity and composure. Box breathing is an effective stress management strategy used by Navy Seals that you can implement in your daily routine. It goes like this: 4-second inhalation, 4-second hold, 4-second exhalation, 4-second hold, and repeat a few cycles.

Next, the purpose for high-volume is to account for frequent no-shows, cancellations, or reschedules. I factor in that about 10-15% of my patient's for any given day will not actually make their appointment. Despite text reminders, emails, and/or phone calls. Now, some days, they all show up and it's crazy. To that I say, buckle up buttercup and get through it because it won't be like that every day. With systematic planning, it shouldn't matter if all your patients show up or not, start every day off the same way. Review or reset your priorities based on what you see on the schedule or maybe even a weekly review and then update each morning with a quick review. Identify the most critical tasks that need immediate attention and tackle those first. Once those tasks have been prioritized, determine if any of those can be taken on by support staff. Remember, you're not in this alone. If you have support staff or colleagues, don't hesitate to delegate tasks. They can help with paperwork, phone calls, and even some exercises, lightening your load and allowing you to focus on patient care. Evaluate if you can break your day into manageable chunks. Dedicate specific time blocks to patient treatments, documentation, and administrative tasks.

Stick to your schedule as closely as possible to maintain a sense of structure. There is a weekly review sheet in the appendix you may use for identifying patients that will need a date extension, a progress note, a discharge, as well as auditing patient's who are "missing in action" (MIAs) or no-shows without a scheduled next visit.

2

Building Strong Foundations

In the bustling world of outpatient orthopedic physical therapy, it's easy to get lost in the whirlwind of paperwork, schedules, and treatment plans. But always remember, your primary purpose in the clinic is to help people – real people with real lives, not just patients with conditions. This chapter is your compass to navigate the tricky terrain of patient-centered care while balancing productivity and administrative duties.

Patient-Centered Care

In the clinic, you'll quickly learn that patients aren't just cases – they're people with stories, fears, and hopes. Patient-centered care isn't a buzzword; it's the core of what you do. It means tailoring your approach to each patient's unique needs and treating them as partners in their healing journey.

You've at this point spent years in classrooms and possibly clinics, mastering anatomy, therapeutic techniques, and medical knowledge. But now, in the clinic, you'll quickly realize that there's more to it than your textbooks hinted. Patients come to you with more than just physical issues; they bring their stories, fears, and aspirations. You're not just treating a diagnosis; you're helping a person regain their life. So, how do you balance the need for quick, effective interventions with the deep-seated desire to connect with your patients and truly make a difference? The following content lays out real-world strategies to help you do just that.

Every patient is different. Take the time to understand their unique needs, preferences, and goals – whether it's getting back to playing golf, running a marathon, or simply walking pain-free. Make those goals your compass and tailor your interventions accordingly. It's not about a one-size-fits-all approach; it's about providing personalized care. It's not just about treating symptoms; it's about helping people regain their lives. This doesn't mean patient's with different impairments and/or goals shouldn't perform similar or in some cases the same intervention. It just means that you should make an effort to frame the intervention in context of how the intervention relates to their goals and impairments.

Take this example: Two patients are being treated in my clinic, one for unsteadiness of gait/falls risk and the other for low back pain. After performing indicated manual therapy, I ask both patients to engage in a dynamic warm-up to include walking with a knee to chest pull (KTC). I would explain to patient 1 that the KTC promotes weight shifting, glute medius/maximus activation which are integral for improving dynamic stability.

Patient 2 would be educated on how the KTC promotes standing leg iliopsoas lengthening, glute and anterior trunk muscle activation, and increases circulation to the lumbar spine tissues. I would then quickly tie the KTC pull back to one of their goals. This can be repeated for myriad interventions across diagnoses and dysfunctions.

Let me expand a little on goals while on the topic of individuality. Templating goals in the EMR is a solid option. Similar to interventions, many goals can be preset and used across the spectrum. However, make an effort to capture the goals most valued by the patient because these types of goals are really what help determine discharge criteria. Independent of what you think, the patient will have their own idea of what "functional" means. David Deppler was a mentor of mine years ago. David wrote the book "Care Connections", a book some of you reading this may even now when recording functional outcome measures at start of care, progress notes and discharges. David explained to me that patient outcomes are entirely based on the patient's perception of their abilities, not the Physical Therapists. Get a good idea as to what their goals are and their current assessment of their own health. Then consider there beliefs as to what treatment may work best. You'll be surprised by this one. Don't get so focused on Evidence-Based Practice being all about best evidence, i.e. remember EBP is evidence combined with clinical experience and very important here... patient beliefs and values. As you go through treatments, make sure you are including their beliefs. If you can help the patient achieve their goals based on their perceived function independent of what you see clinically, incorporating their ideas into treatment you'll get 5-star reviews on google all day long. If not, they are going to find another clinic. It's happened to me, too many times. Simply ask them what's the most important thing they hope to get out of PT, where are they now with regard to that goal and what they think will get them there.

Furthermore, defined and individualized goal setting absolutely reduces the time you'll spend trying to write a narrative asking for more visits. The insurance company already doesn't want to pay for PT, the referring provider will write new referrals blindly b/c it keeps the patient moving, the patient wants to get better but is concerned about the time and money allocated to rehab, and it's up to you to find that balance. Make life easier for yourself by establishing day 1 what the realistic criteria is for discharge. When they meet it, discharge. If they don't meet the criteria within the expected timeline, write a progress note to explain why. Easy. I have found most insurances like at least one patient-specific goal, i.e. Patient-Specific Functional Scale and one Performance or Body-Region measure, i.e. Berg/TUG and LEFS/DASH, respectively. I like to toss in the SFMA top tier and for sport or industrial athletes, the Functional Movement Screen and the Fundamental Capacity Screen.

Empathy Goes a Long Way

Empathy is the heart and soul of patient care. It's the ability to understand and share the feelings of another person, and it's what transforms physical therapy from a mechanical process into a truly healing experience. In a busy clinic, it can be challenging to carve out time for those meaningful connections, but it's absolutely essential. Patients are often in pain, vulnerable, and seeking reassurance. Empathy helps build trust and a strong therapeutic alliance. When patients feel that you genuinely care about their well-being, they're more likely to be open, compliant, and committed to their treatment. Empathetic care has a positive impact on treatment outcomes. When patients feel heard and understood, they're more likely to engage in their rehabilitation fully. They're also more likely to report their concerns and challenges, allowing you to tailor their treatment plans effectively. Stress of their injury is already an issue, the clinic craziness could be an additive factor, but your empathy can lower their anxiety. The patient will sense the clinic chaos. Patients have come to me for an injury that was being treated by another PT at a different clinic because their last clinic was just a patient mill where they felt like a cash cow. Well let me be very clear here, all high-volume outpatient clinics are mills. My clinic is no different in that regard. However, simple gestures, like a warm smile, a kind word, or a genuine inquiry about their well-being, can go a long way in reducing their stress.

In a busy clinic, aka "patient mill", it's easy to rush through conversations with patients. Slow down and actively listen. Make eye contact, nod to show you're engaged, and ask open-ended questions that invite them to share their thoughts and feelings. This simple act makes a world of difference. You can spare a few moments to connect with each patient if you have adequately prepared for the day, maintain good communication with your support staff, have templated treatments and smart phrases. Your body language speaks volumes. Use open and inviting body language, such as facing the patient, maintaining a relaxed posture, and using a warm and welcoming smile. These non-verbal cues convey empathy without slowing down the process. Patients want to feel that their emotions are valid. When they express frustration, fear, or pain, acknowledge these feelings. Say something like, "I can see this is really challenging for you, and it's okay to feel frustrated." Validating their emotions builds trust. Even in a high-volume clinic, find ways to personalize your care. Document brief personal details about your patients, such as their hobbies, family, or upcoming events. These notes can show that you genuinely care about them as individuals. Empathy doesn't mean sacrificing time. Rather, it's about making the most of the time you have. As you barrel through the clinic between patients, the front desk, the bathroom, the snack area, or wherever you pingpong, talk to patients, even if they're not your patient. A simple, heartfelt comment, like "I can see you're working hard; keep it up," takes seconds but means a lot to the patient.

I have experienced, and you'll inevitably encounter this as well, patients who get emotional or start to cry during their physical therapy visits. This can be a challenging situation, especially when you have a packed schedule and a line of patients waiting. In a clinic bustling with activity, it's essential to establish an environment where patients feel safe expressing their emotions. Start by setting the tone with your welcoming demeanor, an empathetic introduction, and an assurance that this is a judgment-free space. Let them know it's okay to share their feelings. Go back to your active listening and make eye contact, nod to acknowledge their emotions, and use verbal cues like "I'm here for you," or "I'm listening." These are called Empathy Statements and help them feel heard and valued. You can find more empathy statements in the appendix. You may have a tight schedule, but giving the patient a moment to compose themselves can go a long way. A simple "Take your time; I'm here when you're ready" shows your empathy without compromising efficiency. During emotional moments, it's crucial to manage your time wisely. If a patient needs more time than initially scheduled, adapt your plan on the fly. This might mean delegating some documentation tasks or incoming patients to support staff. Go speak to those patients walking in the door, you don't need to give them specifics but be transparent with them. Explain you need a few moments with a patient that's having a rough time and needs additional attention. Ask the patients coming in to get started with their warm-up (bike, UBE, etc.), then your support staff can take them from there.

While empathy is vital, it's also essential to set clear boundaries. Let the patient who is crying or emotional know that you're there to support them, but the session needs to continue. This balanced approach conveys your understanding and professionalism. Ask them how they feel about continuing for the day. "Patient, I am here for you and want to support you. I also want to help your knee, shoulder, etc to get better. What do you think would be most helpful right now? Do you want to continue with PT today or do you want to call it a day? There's no right or wrong here, you do what's best for you". Remind the patient that their care is a collaborative effort. Express your commitment to helping them achieve their goals, even if it takes time. This keeps the focus on their progress and empowers them.

After emotional encounters, take a moment to reflect. Consider if there were any areas where the process could be streamlined. Continuous improvement ensures that balancing empathy and efficiency becomes second nature. I have found treating patients in a closed treatment room often invites emotional situations. I would often fall behind on the schedule, not keep up with my notes and lose contact with other patients in the clinic. In an effort to handle these situations more effectively, I have stopped treating patients behind closed doors. This has worked well for me but this doesn't have to be your solution.

Balancing empathy with efficiency can be emotionally draining. Practice self-care to maintain your own emotional resilience. Find moments to destress and refocus, ensuring you have the emotional resources to provide empathy when needed. Try not to take on your patient's emotions. You are not a sociopath for moving on after that encounter.

Empathy is not about spending hours listening to patients' life stories but rather about the quality of the interaction. Patients will remember how you made them feel, even in a short encounter. Implementing empathy in a high-volume clinic doesn't need to slow you down. It can, in fact, enhance patient outcomes and create a more fulfilling experience for both you and your patients. In the busy world of outpatient orthopedic physical therapy, empathy is your secret weapon for success.

Establishing Trust and Rapport

Trust is your currency. Patients need to trust you before they'll follow your guidance. Building rapport is an art. You'll learn to connect with people from all walks of life, make them feel heard, and earn their trust through your actions, not just your words. Bear in mind, speed doesn't mean rushing. Yes, you'll have a busy schedule, but that doesn't mean you have to rush through treatments. While efficiency is key, it's equally important to ensure your patients feel heard and valued. Spend a few extra moments at the beginning of each session to ask how they're doing and what their goals are. Listening isn't just about hearing words; it's about understanding the person behind them. Patients will share their fears, frustrations, and victories. Learn active listening techniques that let patients know you're not just listening; you're truly hearing them. Make eye contact, nod in understanding, and ask open-ended questions. Let patients express themselves, and really hear what they're saying. Then write brief notes in your chart to prompt future conversation that makes them feel valued as a human, not just a patient. This means, you should at least take a 5-second glance at the prior note before walking up to the front to grab the patient or engage them at the recumbent bike, UBE or elliptical.

Additionally, empathy goes a long way to developing rapport. Show genuine empathy. Patients appreciate it when they feel like you understand their pain and challenges. Share a kind word, a reassuring smile, or even a simple "I'm here for you." It can make a world of difference. It's easy to try to relate to a patient's pain or emotional state by diving into a comparative story, i.e. "I know how you feel, once I...." but try to avoid this situation. This may come off as a "1 up" story. Just listen and ask them how you can help.

Effective Communication Skills

Your communication skills will be tested daily. You'll explain complex medical concepts in plain language, convey empathy without sounding scripted, and be the bridge between patients and their healthcare team. Effective communication isn't optional; it's your superpower.

Be transparent about what patients can expect from their treatment. Discuss the timeline, potential setbacks, and the role they play in their own recovery. Setting realistic expectations helps manage frustrations and keeps them motivated. Here's the thing about timelines, everyone at the table has their own. The doc sends patient with a referral for PT 2-3 times per week x 4-6 weeks for patellofemoral pain syndrome, the patient is overweight and works at a warehouse that includes stair climbing, pushing moderately heavy carts and getting out of a forklift throughout the day, has a $40 co-pay, and your assessment indicates patellar tendinopathy, stiff posterior thigh extensibility, overall deconditioning, and history of episodic low back pain all of which would require 12-16 weeks of progressive rehab and performance training for return to work without increased symptoms. You need to acknowledge all of these with the patient so a clear plan and expectations can be established.

Additionally, communicate and educate while treating your patient. While you're performing manual interventions or the patient is performing an exercise/activity, explain what you're doing or what they are doing and why. Use plain language and visual aids if necessary. Educated patients are more likely to be engaged in their own recovery.

In the midst of the clinic's whirlwind, always remember why you chose this path. It's not just a job; it's a calling to help people feel better, return to their passions, and live life to the fullest. The paperwork, schedules, and productivity goals are important, but they should always serve the greater purpose of patient-centered care. You're not just a physical therapist; you're a healer, a motivator, and a partner in your patients' journey to recovery. Embrace this role, and you'll build a strong foundation for a fulfilling and meaningful career in outpatient orthopedic physical therapy.

3

Time Management

Scheduling Strategies: The Calendar Conundrum

When it comes to scheduling in a busy orthopedic clinic, it's like trying to wrangle a herd of cats. You've got a ton of patients to fit into your day, but you can be sure that some of them won't show up or will want to change their appointments, and if your clinic is like mine you may get walk-ins. It's a real brain teaser, but here's a look at a couple of scenarios to help you navigate this appointment puzzle.

Scenario 1: The Ever-Changing Rodeo

Imagine a clinic that has about 30 patients on the schedule each day. But, here's the kicker – the clinic staff know from experience that about 10% of the patients are going to flake out or need to reschedule. So, they're really dealing with around 27 patients a day.

Now, let's talk money. The clinic usually gets about $100 per patient, which should add up to a sweet $3,000 a day.

But, when they factor in those no-shows and cancellations, they're looking at around $2,700 in reality. However, the not so glamorous part of running an orthopedic clinic involves keeping the lights on, paying the bills, and having some leftover for your rainy day fund. This clinic, like any other, has its own costs to cover. We're talking rent for the swanky clinic space, utilities to keep the lights on (literally), salaries for the hardworking staff, insurance, and all that fancy equipment you use to work your magic. Every month, these expenses stack up. Let's say their total monthly expenses weigh in at $30,000. That's a pretty penny, right? Now, if you're doing the math, you'll see why it's crucial to keep the money coming in. If they want to break even, they need to make at least $30,000. But they don't just want to break even; they want to make a profit. Remember, this clinic is planning for around $2,700 a day in revenue, factoring in those sneaky no-shows and reschedules. With some quick math, that's roughly $67,500 a month. Now, the game changes when you factor in those uncooperative insurance plans that don't play nice with double booking. That means for every patient, they can only bill for the face-to-face time they spend. So, they need to make the most of every minute they have with a patient to make ends meet. Running a clinic isn't just about treating patients; it's about balancing the books, making sure your business stays in the green, and delivering top-notch care all at the same time.

The Fix for Scenario 1

To tackle this problem, they have a little trick up their sleeve: they double book. This was super scary for me when I first accepted this strategy, but not every hour is double booked and there are patients who can handle it on their own. With help of the support staff – the often unsung heroes of the clinic - exercise technicians, the clinic can keep running smoothly. But here's the hitch – not all insurance companies play nice with double booking and only pay up for face-to-face time.

For those insurance plans that don't dig double booking, you have to make every minute count during the face-to-face time. And just to be clear, just because you aren't face-to-face and not billing for services, doesn't mean they can't work with an exercise tech. These people need to get better and will benefit from the full hour versus only 30 or 40 minutes. Alternate bookings with insurance payers who allow billable time while supervising the treatment of the other patient who is working with the tech. This way, they've got their bases covered and can justify every billable service. Patients with insurance plans that are a double booking "no go" would require group coding in this instance and then you could bill the full treatment units for the patient with an insurance plan that allows for double booking.

8:00AM	Patient 1 (federal payer)	
8:30AM	Patient 2 (non- federal payer)	Patient 3 (non- federal payer)
9:00AM	Patient 4 (federal payer)	

In the above example, the 8:30 slot is double booked. Federal plans do not permit billing for time not patient facing. I would spend approximately 30-40 minutes with patient 1 and bill for my direct care. Patient 2 and 3 would start their visit with an exercise technician that I would have rounded with earlier in the day. While directly working with Patient 2 or 3, I then bill the time Patient 1 is in the clinic as group therapy. Reimbursement for group therapy is small but better than nothing and it's the ethical thing to do. Once patient 4 comes into the clinic, they have a federal payer and the same rules apply as Patient 1. I would bill for group time for Patient 4 while I work with Patient 2 and 3 for a bit. Once I transition to Patient 4, I will start to bill for direct care. I am still able to bill an hour's worth of units for Patient 2 and 3. See below for an example of the codes used, units billed for each patient and the gross earnings (contracted rates may vary by region and company) for each visit.

Patient	Procedural Code	Units	Total Earning
1	Manual Therapy 97140 ($26.52) Therapeutic Exercise 97110 ($28.82) Group Therapy 97150 ($17.68)	1 1 2	$90.70
2	Manual Therapy 97140 ($26.52) Therapeutic Exercise 97110 ($28.82) Therapeutic Activity 97530 ($36.02)	1 1 2	$127.38
3	Therapeutic Exercise 97110 ($28.82) Therapeutic Activity 97530 ($36.02)	1 3	$136.88
4	Therapeutic Exercise 97110 ($28.82) Therapeutic Activity 97530 ($36.02) Group Therapy 97150 ($17.68)	1 1 2	$100.20

Scenario 2: The Crazy Mix

In another clinic, it's even more of a circus. They've got 40 patients scheduled, but a whopping 15% of them don't show up or want to reschedule. That leaves them with around 34 patients to treat each day. Money-wise, they usually rake in about $80 per patient, which should mean $3,200 a day. But when they factor in those pesky cancellations, they're left with around $2,720.

Here's the twist – lots of their patients have insurance plans that don't allow double booking, making it tricky to amp up their efficiency.

The Fix for Scenario 2

For these folks, the workaround is to be smart about their

scheduling. They keep some buffer slots open for last-minute appointments, giving them room to handle urgent cases and plug the gaps left by no-shows. They're also big on educating their patients about the importance of showing up and sticking to their treatment plans. They send reminders through texts, emails, and phone calls to make sure everyone's on the same page.

Documenting Efficiently: The Paperwork Marathon

In the clinic, paperwork is as much a part of your day as therapy sessions. Efficient documentation isn't just about typing; it's about being a wordsmith, a data entry pro, and a detective all at once. You'll chart assessments, treatment plans, and progress notes with the speed of a seasoned reporter on a deadline. Accuracy is your watchword, but speed is your ally. You'll uncover shortcuts and hacks to conquer the mountain of documentation that looms before you daily. Early I addressed the fact you're going to see your fair share of patients in a day. Some days, it might feel like you're sprinting from one treatment to the next. And what happens in between? That's right, it's time for the dreaded paperwork… or you stay up late after hours to finish up.

EMR (Electronic Medical Record) systems can be your best buddy. They often come with templates and smart phrases that can save you tons of time. Use these to your advantage. Customize your templates to match your treatment approach, and you'll be amazed at how much time you save. You can find examples of smart phrases in the appendix. Whatever you choose to write, my smart phrases or your own, just keep in mind that less is often more. Your notes don't need to be novel-length. They should be concise and clear, focusing on the essentials. Instead of writing paragraphs, use bullet points or short sentences. I remember sweating bullets in school and during my clinical rotations when it came to writing notes. I felt like I needed to document everything and do so in a format that was professional. I started out my career doing the same thing but reality checked me and that style of documenting isn't sustainable. No way my notes stand up in class these days (sorry Dr. Labec!), but I try to strike the balance of getting in the important stuff for all the patients I see in a day and going home without my computer. Develop a systematic approach to documenting. Create a routine where you follow the same pattern for each type of documentation. This not only speeds up the process but also ensures you don't miss critical information. This next point is vital... Try not to wait until the end of the day to document everything. Do it as you go. After a session (I try to do my notes during the session) with a patient, jot down key points while the details are fresh in your mind. This can save you hours of late-night paperwork sessions. Complete your notes as you go but leave them open. At the end of your day, have a routine for reviewing your notes. It's easier to catch and correct errors when the patient's visit is still fresh in your memory. If you have support staff like PTAs or exercise technicians, ask them to assist with documenting some parts. For example, I ask my technicians to write down quick notes on the printed out flow sheet for exercises and activities they observed while I treat another patient. If you don't print out flow sheets, consider giving them access to your computer to make these notes. Just make sure you read through those notes before signing off! I'll say it again, have a well-organized workspace. Make sure you can easily access the documents you need. Time spent searching for paperwork is time wasted. PT's are notorious for having paperwork (and snacks) everywhere!

Full disclosure: some days, I'm absolutely cooked from the first patient on and I have no idea who or what I am by the end of the day let alone get all my notes done. As the saying goes, "It is what it is". However, by developing the discipline to use smart phrases, keeping things short, document while treating (or right after), and putting (and keeping) things in their place, I'm done with my notes at the end of the workday more often than not.

Prioritizing Patient Care: The Urgency Dilemma

In a high-volume clinic, every patient matters... but not all of them require the same level of hand holding, manual therapy or supervision. You've got patients with urgent issues, those with chronic conditions, and some who need routine follow-ups. People who've just had surgery need a lot of attention right out of the gate. They might be dealing with wounds, pain, and the whole post-op shebang. Some folks are dealing with recent injuries or sudden flare-ups of existing problems. They need you to swoop in like a superhero and save the day. Then, you've got your regulars with chronic stuff that needs managing, but they're not in a massive rush. Finally, there's the group that's on a schedule, needing check-ins and updates. So, how do you handle this mix while giving everyone top-notch care?

Start your day by sorting your patients based on their urgency.

Know who needs help ASAP, like post-op folks or someone in agony. Write it on the printed schedule for your support staff to see when you will likely need help covering other patients in the clinic. Now, for those who don't need a red-alert response but are on a routine follow-up, consider double-booking as discussed earlier. That means having two patients scheduled at the same time. One can work with you while the other gets attention from a support teammate. This trick helps you make the most of your time, but remember, some insurance types don't play nice with double-booking. Keep the conversation flowing with your support crew, exercise techs, and PTAs. Be clear about what each patient needs and what role everyone plays in their care. Teamwork is the name of the game.

Hold some slots in your schedule for urgent cases. This way, you're ready to swoop in when someone needs immediate attention without throwing your whole day out of whack. At my clinic, we offer free injury screens. We advertise this to all our athletes who tend to use this option when deciding if a trip to the ED or PCP is needed. We can then convert these screens into a formal PT eval with follow-up visits. To do this, I keep a couple spots with only one patient booked instead of double booking the whole day. Despite all the planning, stuff happens. Stay adaptable. Adjust things on the fly to make sure every patient gets what they need without you going bonkers. Before each week kicks off, give your schedule a once-over. Make sure you've got enough time for the different types of patients. Being proactive keeps the chaos at bay. While you're all about putting out fires, don't forget the slow burners. Patients with chronic issues need your steady hand and care too. The urgency dilemma is like a daily obstacle course. But with some smart planning and the ability to roll with the punches, you can make sure every patient gets top-tier care without feeling like you're about to pull your hair out. You can find my daily and weekly checklist for managing the urgency dilemma in the Appendix.

The Urgency Dilemma

IN A HIGH-VOLUME CLINIC, EVERY PATIENT MATTERS... BUT NOT ALL OF THEM REQUIRE THE SAME LEVEL OF HAND HOLDING, MANUAL THERAPY OR SUPERVISION.

Start your day by sorting your patients based on their urgency. Know who needs help ASAP, like post-op folks or someone in agony. Write it on the printed schedule for your support staff to see when you will likely need help covering other patients in the clinic.

Now, for those who don't need a red-alert response but are on a routine follow-up, consider double-booking as discussed earlier. That means having two patients scheduled at the same time. One can work with you while the other gets attention from a support teammate.

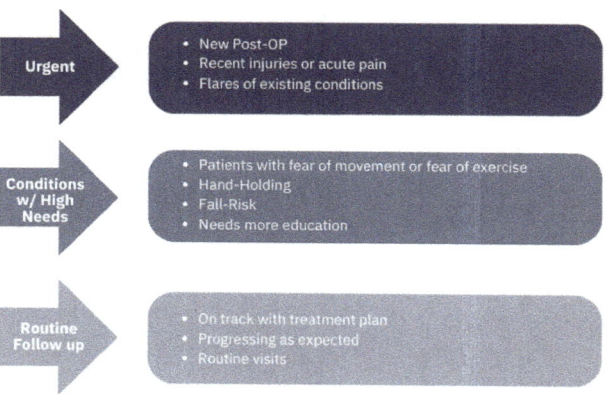

Urgent
- New Post-OP
- Recent injuries or acute pain
- Flares of existing conditions

Conditions w/ High Needs
- Patients with fear of movement or fear of exercise
- Hand-Holding
- Fall-Risk
- Needs more education

Routine Follow up
- On track with treatment plan
- Progressing as expected
- Routine visits

4

Clinical Skills for Success

Assessing Orthopedic Conditions

Now in the world of outpatient orthopedic physical therapy, assessing orthopedic conditions isn't a walk in the park. It's a bit like juggling, but sometimes jogging on a trail blindfolded while being chased by something scary. You have to handle things differently for post-op patients than those with mysterious, gradual pains. Let's break it down and find some practical strategies for your assessment game.

When you're dealing with post-op patients, things are a tad more straightforward. You got surgical reports, images, post-op protocol and a timeline to help you out. You can follow a more specific path here. Check for any complications, assess how they're healing, and customize a treatment plan for their surgery.

But when the patient sitting in front of you indicates their injury of unknown mechanism has been present for, well, an unknown length of time, could be 2-3 months or 2-3 years, who knows... definitely not the patient. This patient also doesn't come into the clinic with a very clear referral. This is when you reach into your back pocket and pull out your Sherlock Holmes hat and a tool known as "Occam's razor", not an actual razor. Occam's razor encourages the clinician to keep things simple. The razor says, when you're faced with many possible explanations, the simplest one is usually the right one. If the patient has scapular pain it's likely 1. Scapular dyskinesia or C7 referred pain, it's most likely not cancer or visceral pain. That being said, know your pathology so you're ready to catch that non-mechanical pain. Just don't waste your eval time chasing zebras if you see horses right from the start.

First, and by far the most cliche but dang it's true, is to just listen to your patient. Their story can be your first clue. In particular, what makes it worse or better, in anything? Their medical history is also gold. Watch how they move. How do they sit? How do they walk? These little observations can reveal big hints. Clear any red flags. Then if there's any indication nerves might be involved, i.e. burning, searing, weakness without pain, radicular pain in hands or feet, or simply can't feel hands or feet... then perform a quick neural screen. Bang it out. UE/LE reflexes... not both, just focus on the area of the body you need. Neural compression and tension tests, think Spurling, ULTT A, Cervical Quadrant testing, Slump, ASLR. If there's a fall or trauma in their history, pop out a few ligament integrity tests like the Alar Test, Transverse Ligament Test/Sharp-Purser Test. Learn and lean into your practice guidelines and clusters.

Once your done using special tests to screen (using tests with high sensitivity) for bad things, it's time to make a decision: 1) get the heck out of here and go to the ED (cauda equina, compromised transverse/alar ligament, + UMN signs, concussion, heart attack, CVA.. scary stuff), 2) f/u with your doctor about some things but let's still look at how you move, or 3) all good, let's get to how you move. This is where my book starts to look like a commercial for Gray Cook et al's Functional Movement Screen (FMS) and Selective Functional Movement Assessment (SFMA). I do not have any disclosures here, I am not affiliated with Gray Cook or the FMS company. I have completed hundreds of hours of CEUs related to assessment to iron out a systematic process to move fast but efficient. The FMS/SFMA process works the best for me. I encourage you to take courses from various educational companies: FMS, Gray CAFS and 3DMAPS, PRI, etc and find your process because in a busy clinic, you need answers fast, and you need to have a well practiced exam routine as your guide.

Most patient's present to Physical Therapy with a chief complaint of something hurting. The SFMA consists of a systematic method of observing fundamental human movement patterns and ultimately making a clinical assessment on what is directly and maybe indirectly related to the patient's pain. Each pattern serves a specific purpose, helping you identify major problems or limitations in their movement. These initial patterns are called your top tier patterns, which are then followed by pattern breakouts where individual components of each pattern are explored to determine their contribution to the dysfunctional and/or painful movement. By the end of the SFMA, you should have a pretty good idea of where the issue lies as well as what other areas of the body may be contributing via regional interdependence. If it's deemed safe to treat after history and special test screening, I then take the SFMA results and run them against the Treatment-Based Classification System (TBCS) to further guide effective treatment plans, which just so happens to be the next section (funny how that works!). You also have folks who waltz into your clinic without pain. Well for me, that's where the Functional Movement Screen struts onto the stage. It's similar to the SFMA in that it offers you a systematic approach looking for movement dysfunction. While crafting your plan of care for those without pain, FMS helps you map out the road ahead.

In the appendix, you can find an example of the SFMA, FMS and TBCS. I highly recommend you learn more by enrolling in the SFMA level 1 and 2 courses. Included in the Appendix is a quick case study example of a patient where lumbar test clusters, SFMA and TBCS were combined.

1st Visit **Assessing & Treating**

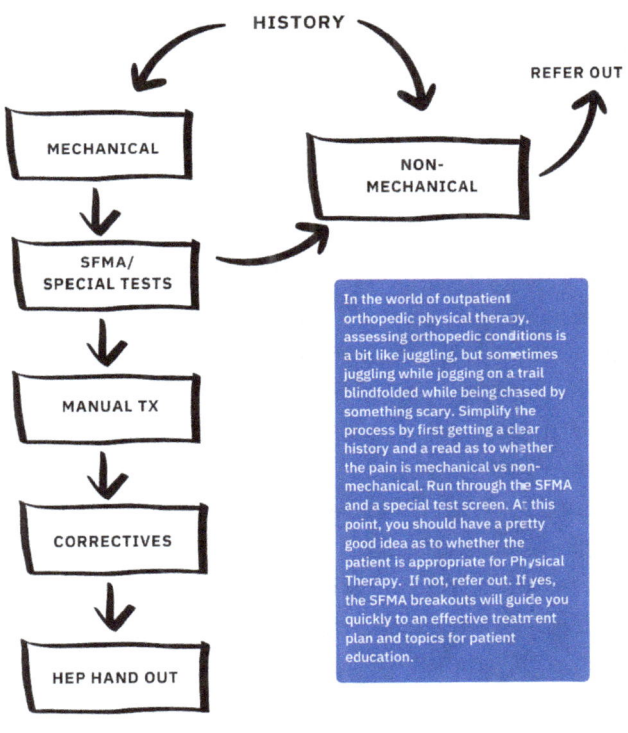

In the world of outpatient orthopedic physical therapy, assessing orthopedic conditions is a bit like juggling, but sometimes juggling while jogging on a trail blindfolded while being chased by something scary. Simplify the process by first getting a clear history and a read as to whether the pain is mechanical vs non-mechanical. Run through the SFMA and a special test screen. At this point, you should have a pretty good idea as to whether the patient is appropriate for Physical Therapy. If not, refer out. If yes, the SFMA breakouts will guide you quickly to an effective treatment plan and topics for patient education.

Creating Effective Treatment Plans

Treatment plans are your roadmap to recovery. Crafting them is an art that combines science and intuition. You'll develop plans that are tailored to each patient's unique needs, considering their goals, lifestyle, and progress. This is where the SFMA and the TBCS come into play. These are your trusty tools that help you dig deep and uncover the underlying issues. With the SFMA, you're checking the body's movement patterns to find out what's funky and the TBCS helps categorize patients based on their symptoms and movement patterns.

Once you know what is wrong and how to classify them, iron out some realistic goals. I lean into the Patient-Specific Functional Scale (PSFS). I do this for two reasons, insurance companies like it and the patient is spoon feeding you goals. I build treatment plans that accomplish what I want for the patient based on my assessment but that can be tied back to those goals. Compliance is pretty dang high if the exercises are relevant and pass what I call the "so what" test, i.e. patient do this squat from the chair without using your hands "so" you can reduce your risk of falling and have greater independence in your home. I would be remiss if I didn't at least make sure to address the fact (from a reimbursement stand point) goals should be Specific, Measurable, Achievable, Relevant, and Time-bound (SMART). The PSFS helps with specificity and relevance but you need to "read the room" to make sure it's realistic (achievable) and if not help the patient adjust their expectations and then include the goals measurement and time frame. Instead of vague objectives, like "reduce pain," aim for something like "Increase thoracic rotation to within normal limits of 50 degrees in 6 weeks to allow for greater functional mobility while driving and head turning".

The exercises in a treatment plan need to be practical and doable, both in the clinic and at home. Think of them as tools for progress. This is where you need to read the room. Don't get wild and crazy with your functional exercise routine if the patient doesn't have the background for it. Additionally, selecting exercises or treatment isn't about reinventing the wheel for every case. You can create a bunch of templates for various orthopedic conditions, each with a different tier of complexity. When you spot these issues, you can steer the patient towards specific exercises from the tiered templates. If you decide to explore SFMA/FMS, you will be shown corrective exercises that you can easily include in your treatment plans. Templates of exercises can be your best friend in this real-world scenario. Here's how it plays out. Start by identifying common orthopedic conditions you often encounter – things like rotator cuff injuries, knee osteoarthritis, or lower back pain. Each of these conditions can have varying degrees of severity and complexity, from mild discomfort to post-surgical rehabilitation. Now, you want to create tiered templates for each condition.

These templates are like the base recipe, and you'll adapt them to fit the unique needs of each patient. The first template, basic complexity, is for patients who are in the early stages of a condition or are responding well to treatment. Exercises in this category are simple, focusing on pain reduction and mobility. This can include range of motion exercises, gentle stretching, and basic strength-building. The second template, moderate complexity, is for patients with a moderate level of difficulty. Exercises here are more challenging, building on the basics. This can involve resistance training, proprioceptive work, and more advanced stretches. The advanced template is reserved for complex cases or post-surgery patients. Exercises are intense, involving advanced strength, stability, and functional movements. Now, you take these tiered templates and make them fit like a glove for each patient. You're not just handing out a one-size-fits-all plan. You're modifying the difficulty and exercises within the template to cater to the patient's condition, goals, and progress. As the patient moves forward, you adapt the template. They might start with the basic exercises and gradually move up the complexity ladder. This is where the art of physical therapy shines, as you balance challenge and safety. If you can find the discipline to establish a core group of exercises for impairments/presentations in your templates and keep on hand a few regressions and progressions for each exercise, adapting the level of complexity becomes even easier. The templates and exercise list will adapt over time but don't keep reinventing the wheel with every single patient. A quote from Jocko Willink, "Discipline equals freedom" and in this case means stick with your templates and exercises and you will find it easier to assess response to treatment, complete notes, grab a snack, and use the bathroom as opposed to spending time wondering "what the heck am I going to do with this patient today or is this patient getting better at their exercises?"

As mentioned earlier in this book, time management in a busy clinic is imperative. Your treatment plans/templates should allow for multitasking, and exercise circuits are one of your secret weapons in this regard. Think of it like a mini workout session, a series of exercises, or tasks that your patients can tackle on their own or with little supervision. It's like a "homework assignment" to help them along in their recovery. While you're working your magic with one patient, others aren't just twiddling their thumbs in the clinic. They've got their circuit to keep them occupied. I have also found that patients like feeling in control of their recovery and when given a circuit, it's like saying, "Here's something you can do to help yourself." It's a confidence boost. While they're on their circuit, it also gives you a breather. You can grab a quick snack, catch up on paperwork, write a note or make a call to a referring provider or even dash to the bathroom without feeling like you're leaving them hanging.

To integrate circuits, first identify a set of exercises that fit within your patient's tiered treatment plan. These should be exercises the patient is already familiar with, as safety and proper form are crucial. Lay out the circuit in a simple and straightforward way. You don't want them scratching their heads, wondering what to do next. They should record what they've done and how they felt during the exercises. It's essential for tracking their progress. You can also have your exercise tech's help with intra-session tracking. When appropriate, switch it up a bit. Let them do different circuits on different days. Additionally, patient's want to feel like they are getting a workout and not just rehab. Incorporate core stability exercises even if they have an ankle injury, incorporate legs into their circuit while addressing a shoulder problem. Movement is medicine and if your patient is moving and breaking a sweat in PT, psychologically they will feel closer to full function.

You can find in the appendix a case study that lays out an example of a treatment plan with templates exercises and use of circuits. I encourage you to read more from renowned Strength and Conditioning Coach and Author Mike Boyle to learn more about program design. You can also check out more circuits for different injuries and presentations at my website, www.deltaperformancerehab.com.

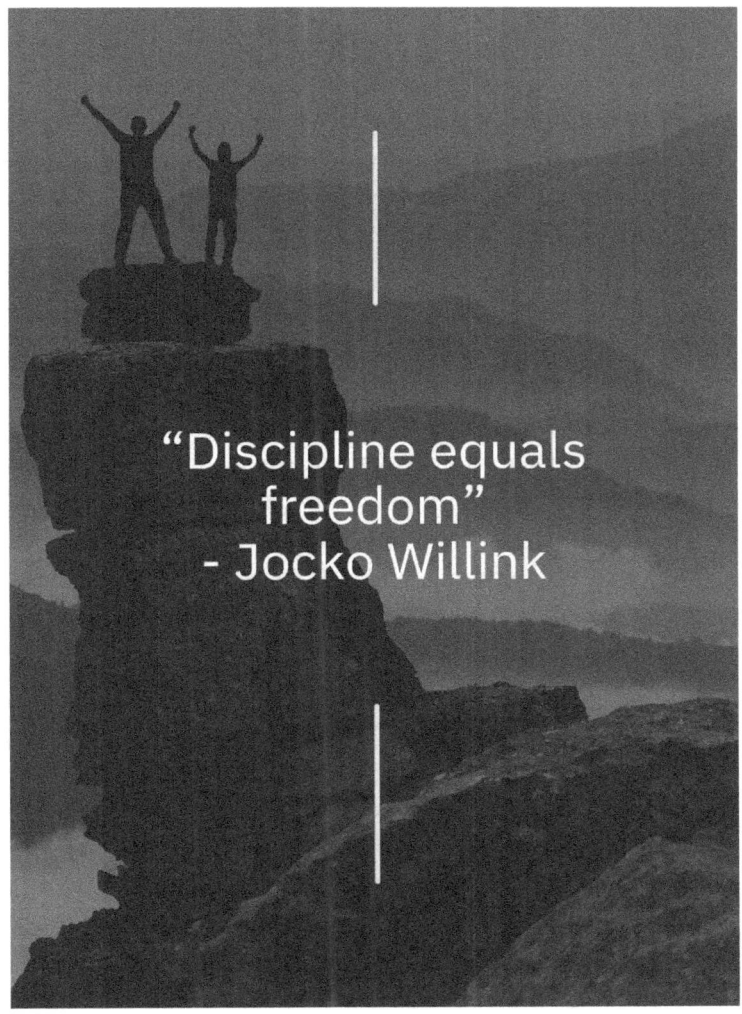

Manual Therapy Techniques

Physical Therapists ride the line between personal trainers (exercise and activities), chiropractors (joint mobilization/manipulation), physicians (red flag management), massage therapists (soft tissue mobilization), and psychologists (yellow flag management). Manual therapy is firmly at the core of the profession and I believe sets us apart. We are given the knowledge to find mobility impairments, address them with our hands and then functionally integrate and correct through exercise and activity with our minds. As much as I appreciate all that manual therapy can offer, it can be a time suck in a busy clinic. Here are my recommendations: don't perform manual therapy behind closed doors, I use the SFMA/test clusters/TBCS to guide my area of focus and anticipated outcome, I begin teaching self-care day one so patients learn how to care for themselves and my hands are free.

First, as described in the prior chapter, run through the SFMA's top-tier movement patterns. It's a quick yet comprehensive screening process to identify movement dysfunctions and home on the potential problem areas. You're not jumping into a full-body manual therapy extravaganza right away, which could be time-consuming and sometimes unnecessary. The SFMA helps establish whether there is joint mobility and/or tissue extensibility dysfunction. Then use your local biomechanical assessment and tissue appraisal to help clarify joint vs tissue. Now, there's a smorgasbord of manual therapy techniques out there you could use once you have identified the area of treatment and what you are treating. We can't cover them all here, but here's the deal: in a busy clinic, a combination is often your best friend. Different patients respond to different techniques. No easy way around that. Sometimes you just need a quick mobilization, and the patient can continue with their exercises or circuits while you do your thing. Other times, you might need a longer manual therapy session, or you want to teach the patient self-care techniques for mobilization. This is where you can lean on your support staff or circuits. While you're providing manual therapy, they can ensure the other patients are on the right track with their exercises and activities.

Once manual therapy has improved joint mobility and reduced tissue restrictions, you transition into functional exercises. But here's where it gets exciting. These exercises aren't generic; they're designed to address the patient's specific issues. Let's use the shoulder as an example. If the SFMA pinpointed a shoulder joint mobility problem, your functional exercises focus on improving shoulder range of motion and strength. Then immediately introduce functional exercises directly complementing what the manual therapy accomplished, i.e. arm bar rolling, ¼ Turkish get, half kneel windmill, bird dog, etc. Remember to circuit those exercises and you'll have time on your side. This synergy between manual therapy and functional exercise is your secret sauce. It's what sets your treatment apart. You're not throwing random exercises at the patient and hoping they help. You're crafting a tailored plan that aligns with your patient's diagnosis, their physical issues, and their goals. Your goal is to make them independent. Through the careful integration of manual therapy and functional exercise, you empower the patient to manage their condition. You teach them not just how to perform exercises but how to self-manage, and this is where long-term success is cultivated.

Keeping an Eye on Discharge

Now that you're ready to be a treatment plan guru, designing exercise programs that target specific weaknesses and improve functional abilities, bare in mind efficient therapeutic exercise prescription isn't just about what exercises to give, but also about knowing when to let your patients fly solo with their rehab. Prescribing exercises with discharge in mind is like planning a successful road trip. I establish goals based on the SFMA or FMS depending on where the patient is starting, really based on presence of pain with movement. You need a clear destination. Establish objective functional criteria that scream, "You're good to go!" It's like setting up signposts along the way. Here it is again, your trusty SFMA commercial. For those with pain as their chief complaint. The SFMA helps you dig deep into the pain issues and provides you clear guidance on what exercises may be helpful and goals to achieve. If you find the pot of gold at the end of the SFMA rainbow and the pain is gone, it's time to shift gears. As the sessions progress, and pain is resolved, use the FMS during subsequent progress notes. It's like checking the road signs. Is your patient on track? The FMS provides objective feedback that can help you make difficult decisions about whether a patient returns to sport practice, competitive play or work. You can calculate the patient's injury risk score. It's like a blood pressure reading when managing hypertension. You assess their potential for risk or injury when they return to their usual activities. This information is invaluable in making safe discharge decisions.

For those athletes or active individuals whose pain has resolved and their FMS score is good to go, then you can lean into the Foundational Capacity Screen (FCS). It is a part of the FMS educational series and offers a more detailed look at the patient's performance capacities. It's like a pit stop before the race. You check their performance metrics and make sure they're well-prepared for their activities. If any deficits show up in the FMS or FCS, don't stress. This is where you bridge the gap. You can provide additional guidance, exercises, or advice to ensure they're fully prepared to return to their activities safely. Discharge isn't the end; it's a new beginning. You've empowered your patients with the knowledge and tools they need to maintain their health and well-being. Now, they can take control of their journey, whether it's life, work, or sports-related. For those reading this book and are interested in additional streams of clinic revenue, bridging the gap between Physical Therapy and Sports Performance is a solid way of doing that. This would be a cash-based program and largely directed by your FCS results and the patient's sport. You are likely not a skill coach, so don't try to be one in the clinic. All sports share similar dependence on basic human movements, and your goal bridging the gap with sports performance is to enhance these movements through progressive loading and conditioning. Source this out to an exercise tech or PTA with a NSCA CSCS background or hire a strength coach to keep in house for this purpose. Market your program to local sports programs, high school athletics, etc.

5

Collaborative Care

Inter-professional Relationships

In the clinic, you're part of a healthcare orchestra. Inter-professional relationships are the harmonious notes that make it all work. From nurses to surgeons, you'll collaborate closely with a diverse team, ensuring that every patient's care is seamlessly coordinated. Now.. the real world: many physical therapists in outpatient orthopedic clinics, likely you reading this, do not have doctors just around the corner. So, you've got to be extra savvy. Limited access to referring providers is a challenge, but it doesn't mean you can't build these crucial relationships. Sending short, personalized thank you letters to the providers who refer patients to you after you have completed the initial examination is a simple yet effective way to establish and maintain relationships. It's like a digital handshake. These letters acknowledge the provider's trust in your expertise and can lead to more referrals down the line. It takes just a few minutes but goes a long way. Keep a stack of Thank You cards with your logo on the front and your business card attached on the inside. Key part here... hand write your message! This makes you seem more like a real person in the eyes of the provider. Your thank you notes should be short and you don't have to reinvent the wheel. Have a few templated phrases you can use in your note with areas for personalization to the provider and patient. Set up a google doc (or whatever program you like) to keep track of referring providers and the last date of the last "touch" you had with that provider via phone call, stopping by their clinic, sending them a thank you note, dropping off referral pads (this one's almost obsolete with electronic referrals but I still have a few providers out there using them).

The progress notes are often like the report card of your care. Handing a printed copy to the patient, with your business card attached, is a brilliant move. It's your way of showing referring providers that you're proactive and open for collaboration. When patients carry your notes to their next visit, it's like you're sending your recommendations right to the provider's desk. It also empowers your patients. They have a clear summary of their progress, which is super useful when talking to their doctors. They become your advocates. If it's not time for a progress note or update in plan of care, provide the patient with a quick letter written directly to the provider regarding the patient's status, in particular if you have any concerns.

Another way of building relationships is to organize luncheons with providers. Call their clinic or stop by when the schedule lightens up and ask if they do luncheons. Organizing a quarterly in-service is a great way for learning and networking, but without the intimidation factor. You can choose a relevant orthopedic topic and invite local providers as well as patient's. They get to learn about new trends, techniques, or research in orthopedics. You're providing value to them, which they'll appreciate. It's a great way to foster relationships. When providers and patients attend, it creates a sense of community around your clinic. These in-services are likely going to take place after hours, so make the people happy by carving out space in the budget to spring for a few different local beers or wines and dinner. Quarterly in-services don't have to be all formal. You can host at your clinic or consider casual gatherings at a local coffee shop. It's a relaxed way to build relationships. Keep conversation loose, try to talk about the neighborhood, share stories, and discuss health topics – no ties required. These gatherings, a.k.a. networking opportunities may provide you an opportunity to directly exchange contact information with referring providers you meet there.

Effective Communication with Physicians

Maintaining efficient and effective communication with referring providers is a game-changer for busy physical therapists in high-volume clinics. You see, when you keep your interactions concise and to the point, it saves you precious time. No lengthy back-and-forths, just the essential updates. Plus, if you've got direct contact information for those referring providers, it streamlines the process even further. You don't have to go through layers of admin or voicemail mazes, which means you can focus more on your patients and less on phone tag.

The beauty of these smooth lines of communication is that it creates a strong network of support. When your referring providers know they can rely on you for clear and timely updates, they're more likely to send more patients your way. In a high-volume clinic, the last thing you need is a bottleneck in the referral pipeline. And don't forget the personal touch. Saying "thanks" and showing appreciation goes a long way. It's like greasing the wheels of the healthcare machine – things run smoother when everyone's working together. In a busy clinic, a well-oiled machine is what you need to get through the daily rush and ensure the best care for your patients.

Being on top of your communication game with referring providers not only saves you time but also strengthens your clinic's reputation and ultimately leads to better outcomes for your patients. It's a win-win situation that every busy physical therapist should aim for.

Consultations and Referrals

In a busy high-volume clinic, having reinforcements, especially for new grads, is like having a lifeline in a fast-paced and litigious world. Whether a newbie to clinical practice or seasoned therapist making a shift to a greater patient load, managing patients in a high-volume clinic can and will get overwhelming if you don't take time to invest and build your team.

When you need reinforcements with a complex patient whose condition seems to fall outside your primary expertise, having a specialist or mentor to lean on is important. Knowing when to refer a patient for a consultation is a superpower because it ensures they receive the best possible care and you... CYA. This is where ego needs to get checked. You're not expected to know it all, especially in a high-volume clinic, so don't pretend to know it all. There can be an aspect of "fake it 'til ya make it" in clinical practice; however, the golden rule is "when in doubt refer out". Understanding your limits is crucial and allows you to set boundaries, which in turn helps to avoid burnout. You can't be the hero for every patient, every time. Sometimes you need backup. And that's okay – it doesn't make you any less of a skilled therapist. In fact, it shows you're committed to your patients' well-being.

Teamwork in Patient Care

Like your referral network discussed in the last section, foster an internal clinic team environment so each clinician and staff member feels supported. When the clinic is bustling and appointments are stacked, it can and will get crazy. Teamwork kicks in during these times. It can feel like playing zone defense in sports, where you keep an eye on your teammates and help out when needed. For example, if a colleague is busy with a hands-on treatment, and their other patient seems lost or has that "I have a question" look on their face, you step in to guide them.

Teamwork isn't limited to colleagues. It includes everyone in the clinic, from administrative staff to exercise techs. By dividing tasks and communicating well, you ensure that no one is overwhelmed. First, encourage open and honest communication. Your team should feel comfortable asking questions and raising concerns when they face challenges. It's essential to establish roles based on each team member's strengths and expertise. Some may excel in scheduling, while others are skilled at designing exercise programs. Assigning roles that align with their abilities can enhance efficiency.

Setting priorities is another key aspect. Admin staff should have a clear understanding of which tasks are most critical, especially when it comes to scheduling patients with urgent needs (refer to the urgency worksheet in the appendix". Provide daily, weekly, and monthly checklists to help your team stay organized and manage their workload effectively. Proper training is essential, ensuring that your admin staff and exercise techs are well-versed in how your clinic operates. Also, make sure to cross train your staff. Inevitably, a front desk coordinator or an exercise tech will call out sick and leave the clinic short on staff. Or simply, the clinic gets so busy that the front desk coordinator, exercise tech or PT/PTA need to jump in to answer the phone, schedule a new eval, cancel/reschedule a visit, talk about billing, etc. You are only as strong as your weakest link. I'm not saying everyone needs to know the nitty gritty fine details of each other's job. That is unrealistic. However, task each non-provider staff member to come up with a list of "the basics" for their job and have them provide a quick inservice with the list during a staff meeting. Review this at each meeting. This will add strength and flexibility to your team's skill set and outward appearance to your patrons.

Consider automating routine tasks, such as appointment reminders, billing, and patient communications. Your EMR should already do this. Automation not only reduces the workload but also minimizes the risk of errors. Realism is vital in workload management. Be sure not to overburden your staff with unrealistic expectations. Encourage them to take regular breaks to prevent burnout, even short pauses can help them stay focused and productive.

Cultivate a sense of teamwork among your staff, where everyone is willing to lend a hand when a team member is overwhelmed. Having the right tools and resources at their disposal is critical to enhancing efficiency. Ensure they have the resources they need to get the job done as your clinic's needs evolve. Establish a feedback loop that allows your staff to share their experiences and suggest improvements. This not only identifies areas that may need attention but also allows for ongoing enhancements. Express your appreciation and recognition of their hard work, as it can boost morale and contribute to a positive work environment. Most likely, you will have staff that are like most humans, scared of confrontation even when you insist the feedback is helpful. Try using an anonymous survey via survey monkey to take a pulse on staff satisfaction and self-efficacy with their work environment. Provide an open dialogue at staff meetings about the results of the survey and be genuine with your interest to address these issues. Ask if anyone has input on how to solve these issues. Changing clinic flow can be met with resistance when the change is passed down. Conversely, if it's the clinic staff who come up with the idea, change may occur faster and be met with optimism.

In a fast-paced clinic, teamwork is what keeps things running smoothly and maintains your sanity. Whether it's helping out a colleague or working with others, teamwork is the key to success. By implementing these straightforward tips, you can help your administrative staff and exercise techs manage their workload more efficiently, reduce stress, and maintain a sense of control in the midst of a bustling outpatient clinic.

6

Work Life Balance

Stress Management Strategies

Stress is your constant companion in high-volume clinics. You'll master stress management strategies to keep your cool when things get hectic. Breathing exercises, mindfulness, and knowing when to take a moment are your allies.

When the clinic is buzzing, and you've got a million things on your plate, take a moment to focus on your breath. Deep, slow breaths can calm your nervous system and clear your mind. Try the 4-7-8 technique: inhale for a count of four, hold for seven, and exhale for eight. Box breathing is another simple and handy technique you can use. U.S. Special Operators use box breathing to help reduce stress during combat. If it works for special forces under extreme stress, you may find it also helpful with clinic stress. Just find a quiet spot, like your office or a calm corner, and sit or stand comfortably. Then, inhale through your nose for four seconds, hold your breath for another four seconds, exhale through your mouth for four seconds, and finally, hold your breath again for four seconds. This structured approach helps lower your heart rate and ease your mind. It's like hitting a mental reset button, providing a peaceful pause during a chaotic day.

Mindfulness is another super tool in your stress-busting arsenal. It's all about being in the present moment. When you're knee-deep in appointments, it's easy to start worrying about the next one or stressing over the last. But practicing mindfulness means giving your full attention to what's happening right now. Take a deep breath, really listen to your patient, and focus on the task at hand. It's amazing how this can help you stay calm and collected in the chaos.

Lastly, know when to take a moment for yourself. A quick break between patients, a few minutes to stretch, or even a short walk can work wonders. Don't feel guilty about it; it's essential for your well-being. Stress can sneak up on you, so staying attuned to your body and mind is key. Recognize the signs of stress – like tension in your shoulders or a racing heart – and give yourself a breather when you need it.

Preventing Burnout

When you find yourself feeling emotionally drained or disengaged from your work, it's a red flag for burnout. In those moments, take a step back and reflect on what's causing these feelings. It might be a signal to adjust your workload or find new ways to stay motivated in your profession. Burnout can sometimes be tied to how therapists feel about their ability to help patients and the sense that they can't control the outcomes. By recognizing the signs and actively taking steps to prevent it, you can maintain your passion for helping patients and keep providing excellent care in your high-volume clinic.

There are some really effective ways to handle burnout on a large and small scale. To avoid it on a large scale, remember that you're not a superhero and no one expects you to be one. Burnout is not a sign of weakness but a real issue that many healthcare professionals face. To prevent or treat burnout, try leaning on your colleagues and create a support network within your clinic. It's okay to ask for help. Sharing experiences, challenges, and solutions can be therapeutic and strengthen team cohesion. Getting guidance and mentorship from experienced colleagues can also be a big help when dealing with complex cases.

Along this line, have fun in the clinic, make a point to laugh with your colleagues and patients during the day. Simply smiling can lighten your mood and make the day not seem so stressful. Find something you enjoy and work into your day at the clinic. For example, I take about 30 minutes of my lunch break to practice chipping (golf short game always needs work!) while eating snacks and drinking a cup of coffee. I practice this lunch time ritual nearly everyday. It helps clear my mind for the afternoon. If you build the discipline to systematically assess, treat and document, you will find that the documentation load during lunch time or after hours will be less and you can engage in fun activities instead, i.e. get in a workout, take a nap, meditate, read a book, or chip some golf balls. Which leads me to boundaries. It's important to set work- and personal related boundaries. Stick to them. You need to take regular breaks during the day. Not staying disciplined in your notes can spill over into these times. Don't let it. Personally, you need to get regular exercise, maintain a balanced diet, and get a good night's sleep. You can't do these things if you are working on chart notes at home or late in the clinic. Discipline equals freedom.

Professionally, staying updated on the latest in therapy techniques and research helps therapists become more skilled and confident, which can lead to better patient results. Better patient results means improved therapist self-efficacy and less burnout. Simply put, get back at what you do and you'll likely enjoy doing it more. Attending professional conferences is a solid win in this regard. Mingle with like minded peeps while learning how to be a better PT... and time off from the clinic. Side note here: go to conferences in places that offer activities you like to do. For me: warm beaches!

The last thing I want to say on this topic relates to mindset. Therapists need to understand that they play a crucial role in patients' recovery and should see themselves as facilitators of the healing process. Building a good connection with patients, setting achievable expectations, and teaching them about self-care and home exercises are essential. By embracing your part in the treatment plan and recognizing your expertise, you can boost your confidence and improve patient outcomes. This approach helps fight burnout and makes the job more satisfying in a busy clinic.

Self-Care for PTs

You can't care for others if you neglect yourself. Self-care isn't selfish; it's survival. You will need to establish routines that keep you physically and mentally fit for the demands of the clinic. Physical therapists are on their feet a lot, so regular exercise and stretching are vital. It's not just about patient health; it's your own musculoskeletal health too.

Make exercise a part of your daily routine. Even quick, intense workouts during breaks can help. Focus on strengthening your core, back, and legs to support your work. Pay attention to your body mechanics when working with patients, using proper lifting techniques and maintaining good posture. Stretching and mobility exercises before and after work can prevent stiffness and increase your range of motion. I will often perform warm ups with my patients (yep, in my polo and golf pants) or grab a foam roll and plop down next to a patient and hit some areas I like to work on while my patient is doing their soft tissue work. Schedule regular massages or manual therapy sessions to address muscle tension and imbalances.

Nutrition is low hanging fruit when it comes to self care (see what I did there). Eating a balanced diet and staying hydrated can support muscle recovery. Incorporate stress management techniques like deep breathing or short meditation sessions to reduce tension. Ensure an ergonomic workstation if you spend time at a desk. One strategy worth exploring is intermittent fasting. This approach can help with weight management and overall health. Intermittent fasting alternates between periods of eating and fasting, which can free up time and mental energy. Popular methods include the 16/8 (fasting for 16 hours and eating within an 8-hour window), the 5:2 (eating regularly for 5 days and consuming very few calories on the other 2 days), and the one-meal-a-day approach.

When it comes to macronutrients, balancing your intake of carbohydrates, fats, and proteins is vital. Carbohydrates provide immediate energy, and including complex carbs such as whole grains, fruits, and vegetables can help maintain steady blood sugar levels. Healthy fats, like those found in avocados, nuts, and fatty fish, support cognitive function and energy. Protein-rich foods help to maintain and repair muscle tissue, which is particularly important for physical therapists.

It's also beneficial to consider supplements like vitamin D, omega-3 fatty acids, and B-vitamins to help maintain energy levels, focus, and overall well-being. Staying hydrated throughout the day is equally essential as dehydration can lead to fatigue and decreased concentration. Caffeine is a common tool used to maintain alertness and focus, especially in a high-demand environment like a busy physical therapy clinic. However, it's essential to use it wisely. Moderation is key when it comes to caffeine intake. Consuming too much caffeine can lead to jitters, anxiety, and interfere with sleep, which is counterproductive in managing stress and maintaining focus.

It's generally recommended that adults limit their caffeine intake to around 400 milligrams per day, which is roughly the amount in four cups of brewed coffee.

You can strategically use caffeine by having a cup of coffee or tea when you need a boost in energy and focus. Some physical therapists find it beneficial to time their caffeine intake strategically, for instance, before a busy clinic shift or during an afternoon slump. I have observed energy drinks help with the afternoon slump. If you choose to go this route, I encourage you to read the labels, know what you are drinking and choose healthier natural energy drinks. It's also important to remember that individual tolerance to caffeine can vary, so it's crucial to know how your body responds and adjust accordingly. Make sure you balance out that caffeine with some water, preferably before 7:00 PM at night when you remember you haven't taken a sip of water all day! If you haven't tried caffeinated drinks in the past, I recommend you speak with your primary care provider first.

And on that note, don't be the healthcare worker who thinks because they know about healthcare they don't have to schedule check-ups with healthcare providers to catch and address potential issues early. Be an adult and make appointments with your own providers to address health issues. Oh and follow their advice, that's their wheelhouse.

Finding Work-Life Balance

Maintaining a healthy work-life balance is crucial for the well-being of a busy physical therapist in a high-volume clinic. To achieve this balance, consider implementing various tactics, strategies, and hacks that can free up time for personal pursuits and relaxation. One approach is to explore alternative work schedules, such as compressed workweeks, where you work longer hours on fewer days, allowing for extended weekends. This schedule can provide more uninterrupted time for travel, leisure activities, and hobbies. Also consider reduced work hours overall, like only working 36 or 32 hours per week to achieve a better work-life balance. Before making such a decision, it's essential to assess your financial situation and see if you can comfortably adjust to fewer working hours. This may involve some budget adjustments to ensure that your income aligns with your financial needs. However, the trade-off can be well worth it, as working fewer hours can provide more time for personal pursuits, relaxation, and maintaining a healthy work-life balance. Ultimately, it's about finding the right balance that allows you to enjoy your life outside of work while still meeting your financial responsibilities.

Another strategy is to establish firm boundaries between work and personal life. Set specific times for work, and when those hours end, make a conscious effort to unplug from work-related responsibilities. This can be achieved by turning off email notifications or setting designated times for checking work messages. Additionally, time management techniques, such as the Pomodoro method, can help maintain focus during work hours, making you more efficient and leaving more time for yourself. The Pomodoro Technique is a cool time management trick invented by this Italian guy named Francesco Cirillo back in the '80s. He called it "Pomodoro" because he used a tomato-shaped kitchen timer, which is kind of funny. Here's how it works: you pick a task you want to tackle, set a timer for 25 minutes, which is one Pomodoro, and go all-in on that task. When the timer rings, take a short 5-minute break to unwind. After you've done four Pomodoros, treat yourself to a longer 15-30 minute break. The idea is to split your work into these short, focused bursts, so you get stuff done without burning out. It's like a mini-race against the clock with built-in chill time. You can tweak it to fit your style, but it's a nifty way to manage your time and keep yourself productive.

Lastly, consider delegating tasks or utilizing support staff effectively, allowing you to concentrate on patient care while reducing administrative burdens. Task delegation can be a real game-changer for maintaining a healthy work-life balance. It's all about recognizing that you don't have to do everything yourself, especially when it comes to work tasks. If you're a busy physical therapist in a high-volume clinic, this is crucial. You can delegate tasks like appointment scheduling, administrative work, or even some patient education to support staff or PTAs, if applicable. This frees up your time and mental space for more crucial patient care and helps prevent burnout. Things I delegate also include keeping treatment space clean, clinic laundry, calling the referring provider's office and staying on hold while I treat, set up/breakdown electrical stimulation, and for my personal trainers and strength coaches having them write out sports performance routines for athletes.

Outside of work, you can apply this principle too. Don't hesitate to delegate household chores, childcare responsibilities, or other tasks to family members or consider outsourcing for help when needed. This way, you're not carrying the entire burden on your shoulders and can have more quality time for yourself and your loved ones.

Task delegation isn't about avoiding responsibilities; it's about smartly distributing them to maintain your sanity, reduce stress, and create that all-important work-life balance. Remember, (I'm going to say it again) you're not a superhero, and it's okay to ask for help when you need it. It's a strategy that can help you thrive in both your professional and personal life.

7

Patient Education & Empowerment

Educating Patients About Their Conditions

In a high-volume outpatient orthopedic physical therapy clinic, educating patients about their conditions is of paramount importance for several reasons. First and foremost, it empowers patients to take an active role in their own recovery, which can lead to better treatment outcomes. When patients understand their conditions, they're more likely to adhere to treatment plans, follow home exercise programs, and make necessary lifestyle adjustments, ultimately getting back to doing the things they like doing. However, in a high-volume clinic where time is limited, striking the right balance between providing essential education and maintaining a busy schedule can be a challenging task. The following are some concepts I consider when educating my patients.

First I prioritize by focusing on the most crucial information related to the patient's condition, treatment plan, and self-care. Then I simplify complex medical jargon to make it more accessible to patients. I keep a few visual aids around like anatomical models and diagrams to convey complex concepts quickly and effectively. I have recently started leveraging technology to provide resources, such as videos (educational videos provided by my HEP platform) that patients can access at their convenience to reinforce their understanding.

I also like to break down the educational content into smaller chunks. I provide information in manageable segments during each session to reduce the risk of the patient feeling overwhelming. I ask the patient if they have any questions to create an open environment where patients feel comfortable and supported. I keep handouts up front at the check-in desk area and at the PT desk in the treatment area pre-templated information on common conditions/surgeries/injuries that provide general education. In a time pinch, this can go a long way to sparring me a few extra minutes of redundant printing or internet searching.

Physical Therapists should be careful about over-educating patients. It's crucial to find the right balance. While education is essential, overwhelming patients with excessive information may lead to maladaptive behavior. Read the room on this one and be attuned to the individual patient needs and learning preferences. Some patients may thrive with more detailed information, while others may require a simpler, less detailed approach. Ask them what they prefer. Customizing the education process based on patient receptivity is key to preventing information overload.

Setting Realistic Expectations to Improve Outcomes

Patients often come with high hopes and misconceptions. You'll become a master at setting realistic expectations. It's about ensuring patients understand the journey they're embarking on and the time it may take to achieve their goals. You don't want to dash their hopes and kill motivation, but you also don't want to set expectations so high they'll be disappointed. Striking that balance is your artistry as a physical therapist. You're their guide on the road to recovery, helping them navigate the ups and downs, and that's how you rock it in the real world of physical therapy. Now that you've educated your patients about their conditions, you need to paint a clear picture of what's on the horizon. Setting realistic expectations is their GPS to recovery. When patients know what lies ahead and believe it's doable, they're more likely to engage fully in their treatment. That means showing up, giving their all, and being a partner in their recovery journey.

I'll start with the question of how long a patient will be in Physical Therapy and their prognosis. Often the referring provider writes a script for physical therapy 2-3 days per week for 4-6 weeks, but in reality most patients will have several progress notes and plan of care extensions. Physical Therapy is more of a marathon than a sprint. Biological tissue healing is 6-8 weeks for acute conditions, even longer when we are talking about chronic tissue derangement. Be transparent from the beginning and set the right expectations, you're preparing them for the long haul, making them more likely to stick to the plan. If insurance is going to be a limiting factor, i.e. high co-pay, limited visits per year, auto PIP is low or has run out from seeing other health care providers prior to sitting in your clinic, make sure they are ready for that as well. Not knowing what's coming next can be pretty stressful. By painting an accurate picture of their journey, you're reducing anxiety and stress, which can significantly impact their recovery. Being upfront and honest is a trust-builder. Patients appreciate it when you're not sugar-coating things or making empty promises. Trust leads to better patient-therapist relationships.

Just like with education, open dialogue is key. Explain what they can realistically expect from their treatment. Encourage them to express their goals and concerns. Each patient is unique, and so are their goals. Tailor the expectations to their specific condition and needs. Make sure goals are attainable and measurable. Be honest about the boundaries of physical therapy. Sometimes, full recovery may not be possible, but significant improvements can still be life-changing. I try to tie in my SFMA findings with activities they want or need to get back to doing. When setting those expectations and writing your goals, use clear and plain language when discussing their condition and the treatment process. Keep patients in the loop about their progress and any changes to their plan. A sense of control goes a long way in building realistic expectations. You don't need a finish line to celebrate. Small victories along the way can be motivating and build optimism.

Promoting Compliance

Patient compliance is the key to successful outcomes in a high-volume orthopedic clinic. The challenges of a busy clinic mean you can't be with your patients around the clock, but there are strategies to keep them on the path to recovery. To start, recommend home exercise apps that provide clear instructions and reminders – tell the patient "it's like having a Physical Therapist in their pocket". Additionally, cloud-based monitoring platforms allow you to keep an eye on their progress from afar, ensuring they're sticking to their regimen. WebPT is a helpful cloud-based EMR with built-in extensions that offer HEP development and monitoring. I have the most experience with WebPT but there are so many others. When you do create exercise programs, make sure they align with the patient's lifestyle and interests, such as mimicking movements they enjoy, can make home exercises feel less like a chore. The trick here is to make sure the exercises address deficits noted in your examination and their subsequent visits.

Regular check-ins, even if conducted through telehealth, help maintain engagement and allow you to address any concerns or adjustments needed in their home program. Provide visual aids like videos or images that demonstrate the correct way to perform exercises, creating a handy reference for patients. Setting achievable, measurable goals together, and celebrating even small milestones along the way, can keep patients motivated. Educate them on the benefits of their exercises, helping them understand the 'why' behind each movement.

Moreover, encourage patients to involve their support system, be it family or friends, in their exercise routine to create a strong community of support. In a high-volume clinic, these tactics and tools can act as your watchful eyes when you can't be there in person, guiding patients toward recovery even from a distance. Your role as their coach can make a significant difference in their journey to regain their physical health.

Empowering Patients for Long-Term Health

The ultimate goal with Physical Therapy, in my mind, is to empower patients to provide them the tools they will need on their journey toward independent wellness. In a busy physical therapy clinic where time is often short, it can be difficult to promote lasting health changes without overwhelming them or coming off superficially. To do this, you can offer resources that get straight to the point. For instance, give patients easy-to-understand handouts or online materials that highlight exercise, diet, and stress management basics. Create short exercise routines that they can incorporate into their daily lives, focusing on exercises that deliver the most benefits in the least time.

When setting goals with your patients, keep it simple and aim for just one or two achievable targets per visit. Use motivational questioning techniques to understand what changes patients are ready to make. If applicable, consider using your EMR's Remote Therapeutic Monitoring platform to help with tracking exercise and home exercise compliance. I often instruct my runner's to use wearable fitness trackers for real-time feedback on their steps per minute rate. I give them a steps per minute goal and then we check it together at each visit to see if progress is being made.

You can also provide quick and practical tips for better nutrition and teach them brief mindfulness exercises that can be done in just a few minutes a day. Encourage patients to use health apps and fitness trackers to monitor their progress, celebrating their achievements during sessions. I am a strong advocate of the app Mealime for meal planning. Mealime comes with a free version and then a Pro plan.

Share information about support groups or online communities for added motivation. Finally, consider telehealth appointments for follow-up discussions. These strategies are designed to make it easier for patients to incorporate healthier choices into their daily routines and improve their well-being, even when time is limited during clinic visits.

8

Lifelong Learning

Staying Current with Evidence-Based Practice

I was told in an orientation class for my first job out of PT school that the number of CEU hours for PTs declines over time. They get busy, have a family, travel, get burned out, or some combination of them all. I thought "no way, not me, I love learning!" This next part isn't to brag but to prove my point about learning. I have a Bachelors in Science, a dual Master's in Exercise Physiology and Nutritional Science, a DPT, and my OCS credentials. I love learning. However, life has caught up with me and likely it has or will for you. In a busy high-volume physical therapy clinic, staying updated with evidence-based practice is not just a professional obligation but a practical necessity. It's vital for providing great care and ensuring positive patient outcomes. So how can you, amid your hectic life and schedule, stay on top of the latest research and best practices? One strategy is to leverage online resources. There's a wealth of digital information at our fingertips, including online journals, blogs, and newsletters specific to your area of expertise. Subscribing to these resources keeps you informed about recent research and clinical trials. For instance, you can follow reputable physical therapists, strength coaches, and fitness professionals that regularly publish summaries of new studies, making it easier to stay current. Subscribe to their websites and have the information pushed to you. Same goes for research. Go to PubMed and have several saved search inquiries of topics that interest you pushed to you when articles become available. Delegating administrative tasks to support staff can free up your time for educational pursuits. For instance, they can assist with literature reviews, search for evidence, and even help you keep track of upcoming webinars or workshops relevant to your field. Please, check out my blog and videos at www.deltaperformancerehab.com as it is often updated with information that I come across related to physical rehabilitation, health and wellness, sports performance and personal fitness and nutrition.

Another approach involves active participation in professional associations. Many associations offer members access to valuable resources like clinical practice guidelines and research databases. They also host webinars, conferences, and workshops where you can learn about the latest developments in your field. For example, you might join your regional physical therapy association, attend their annual conference, and engage in discussions about emerging research.

Continuing education is crucial. Some busy clinics provide in-service training, where therapists can share their knowledge and experience with colleagues. If your clinic offers this, it's a great opportunity to learn from your peers. I mentioned earlier that my clinic hosts Functional Thursdays where we simply discuss courses we have attended, new techniques we learned, hash out process improvement for clinic flow, etc. Team meetings at the clinic provide an excellent forum to discuss new research findings and evidence-based practices. If a colleague comes across a relevant study, they can share it with the team. This way, knowledge-sharing becomes a regular practice within your clinic. Outside the clinic, consider enrolling in courses or workshops that pertain to your specialization. Perhaps there's a weekend workshop on the latest orthopedic treatments you can attend. This is where that after hours in-service meeting plays a role. Two birds, one stone. Learn something new and meet other providers in your community. You may not get CEUs for it but continuing education is not only supposed to be about hours.

Additionally, I would recommend incorporating microlearning into your daily routine. For example, if you are a morning person, start your day about 30 minutes before your planned workout. During this time, you can drink your pre-workout supplement and dedicate half an hour to "morning microlearning." This involves reading or watching short educational content, like articles, videos, or podcasts. You can then strive to apply this new knowledge during the day, helping reinforce your understanding and practice of evidence-based care. Integrating evidence-based templates into treatment plans is a practical way to ensure that the most current research informs your practice. These templates, built on the latest research, can serve as a foundation for your treatment plans, making it more straightforward to apply evidence-based care consistently. Each of the templates I use and provided in the appendix reflect a compilation of evidenced-based information.

The Importance of Mentors

In this jungle, mentors are your guiding stars. Mentors are your living, breathing encyclopedias of practical know-how. They've dealt with all sorts of patients, conditions, and surprises that clinic life throws at you. They'll drop pearls of wisdom that no textbook ever could. In the clinic, there's no answer key in the back of the book. Mentors teach you the art of thinking on your feet, adapting on the fly, and finding creative solutions to real-world challenges. Sure, you've learned techniques, but mentors show you how to apply them with the human touch. It's not just about moving limbs; it's about building trust, showing empathy, and communicating effectively. Mentors aren't just therapists; they're career navigators. They'll help you set your professional GPS, offering advice on specializations, certifications, and career growth. The clinic can be a crazy place, and self-doubt can creep in. Mentors provide an ear to listen, a shoulder to lean on, and tales of their own setbacks and triumphs to reassure you that you're on the right path.

Mentorship can take a couple forms. One type of mentorship, the less expensive type, isn't a formal ceremony with a certificate at the end. It's more like finding a gym buddy – you click, you connect, and you learn together. Look for therapists who inspire you, whose approach you admire, and whose knowledge you crave. Approach them, express your eagerness to learn from them, and be ready to soak up their wisdom like a sponge. Remember, mentorship is a two-way street. While you absorb their knowledge, your fresh perspective can also bring new insights to the table. It's a dynamic exchange that benefits both sides. Another type of mentorship, the more expensive type, is a formal arrangement through your company or an outside institution that you pay to have them mentor you. Either way, strongly consider mentorship. I would not be here today if I didn't have help along the way. I have always made a point to keep open dialogue with PT's and PTA's with whom I work regarding examinations and treatments and my thoughts and concerns. Then the next thing I do, the most important, is listen and not get defensive if they correct me. Check your ego before entering a mentorship relationship. For additional reading, check out the book written by Jocko Willink, Extreme Ownership and his follow-up books. I have a complete list of recommended reads in the appendix.

Your growth isn't a solo endeavor. Networking and seeking mentorship from experienced PTs is your path to success. You'll build a support network that guides you through challenges and celebrates your triumphs. Mentorship plays a significant role, too. Experienced therapists can guide their less-experienced counterparts, sharing insights into evidence-based practice. These mentors might, for instance, provide guidance on assessing the quality of research or recommend particular journals to follow. New therapists can benefit greatly from such mentorship.

Pursuing Specializations and Certifications

In regard to specializations and certifications opening career doors, don't buy into it! They really don't. I still make average wages for a PT seeing a crap ton of patient's. Don't romanticize the idea of being a specialist. That said, I firmly believe and buy into that specializations and certifications can help guide your practice patterns and make you more efficient and effective in your work. Below are just a few examples but not an exhaustive list of certifications and specializations.

Functional Movement Systems (FMS) offers a range of certifications focused on movement analysis and corrective strategies. The FMS certification provides you with the tools to evaluate your patients' movement patterns, identify dysfunctions, and develop customized corrective exercises. The Selective Functional Movement Assessment (SFMA), a part of FMS, is particularly beneficial for orthopedic therapists. It enables you to assess movement quality and establish a specific diagnosis quickly. These certifications ensure you can efficiently address the root causes of your patients' issues and provide effective treatment.

The Gray Institute's Applied Functional Science (AFS) certification is another valuable option. This program teaches you how to apply the principles of biomechanics and functional movement in clinical practice. AFS enables you to develop personalized treatment plans based on a deeper understanding of how the body functions. This, in turn, can lead to more efficient and effective interventions for your patients.

For those looking to specialize, the American Physical Therapy Association (APTA) offers board certifications such as Orthopedic Certified Specialist (OCS) or Sports Certified Specialist (SCS). These certifications demonstrate your advanced clinical knowledge and skills in specific areas.

To ensure you stay current, many of these certification programs include regular updates, requiring you to renew your certification every few years. These updates help you stay abreast of the latest research and clinical practices. While pursuing multiple certifications may seem time-consuming, it's an investment in your career that pays off over the long term. Don't forget about your weakest link. Encourage professional development and growth in your support staff as well. They may be hourly employees but it may be worth your while to pay for them to earn a personal training certification or strength coach certification. When I hand off a patient to one of my staff members, I feel more confident in that patient's care knowing my support staff are regularly taking part in professional development.

Charting Your Career Path

Your career isn't static; it's a journey. Charting your career path means setting goals, exploring opportunities, and discovering where your passion and skills align. It's about building a fulfilling and dynamic profession. It allows you to navigate your professional journey, maintain a sense of direction, and make informed decisions about your development. Just like developing a patient's plan of care, identifying your professional goals and aspirations. Consider the areas of outpatient orthopedic physical therapy that interest you the most, performance, sports, pediatrics, etc. Think about whether you'd like to specialize in a particular niche or if you'd prefer a broader clinical role.

Appraise your current skills, knowledge, and experience. Recognize your strengths and areas that need improvement. Knowing where you stand is crucial for planning your path forward. One of my favorite reads is "The Obstacle is the Way", which applies here. If you want to perform more efficiently and effectively in a high-volume outpatient clinic, then you need to target your weak links: your weakness is your way.

Break down your long-term goals into smaller, achievable milestones. For instance, if you aim to become a board-certified orthopedic specialist, your milestones could include gaining experience, taking relevant courses, and preparing for the certification exam. Remember, microlearning can be particularly effective. Dedicate short, focused periods each day to study or engage in skill development. I keep a running list of MedBridge courses I am interested in completing. I organize them in order of priority, or put another way, which course will help me target my weak points first. Then I like to list out which courses provide updated evidence-based practice information on topics I haven't looked at in awhile. Then what courses just look fun. Sometimes to prevent burnout I jump over to the fun list out of order. Also on my phone, I keep a mission statement in which I want my knowledge base to reflect. When deciding on courses, certifications, or specializations, I always run it against my mission statement.

I recommend you create a mission statement as well. It should reflect your core values, goals, and the impact you want to make in your career. To get started, think about why you chose this profession and what drives you. Consider your goals – whether it's achieving certifications, specializing in certain areas, or becoming a leader in your field. Your mission should also incorporate your values, such as patient-centered care, evidence-based practice, or compassion.

Evaluate your current skills and abilities and identify areas you'd like to improve. Your mission should guide you in enhancing your clinical, communication, and leadership skills. Additionally, specify the knowledge tracks you want to follow, which might relate to orthopedics, sports medicine, neurological rehabilitation, or other areas of expertise. Think about the impact you want to have on your patients, your profession, and the healthcare system. It could involve improving patient outcomes, contributing to research, or mentoring future physical therapists.

When drafting your statement, make it concise and inspirational. For example, your mission statement could express your dedication to providing compassionate, evidence-based care and your commitment to professional growth and mentorship. Your mission will help you stay focused, set priorities, and maintain a sense of purpose as you navigate your busy clinic. Review and adjust it periodically to ensure it aligns with your evolving career. Your mission statement will be your guiding star, helping you stay on course and make a meaningful impact as a physical therapist. A template and example are provided in the appendix.

Periodically evaluate your progress and adjust your career path as needed. Reflect on your practice patterns, on your mission statement, and your trajectory. It's essential to remain adaptable and open to change, especially in a fast-paced environment like a high-volume clinic.

9

Celebrate Your Successes

Recognizing Milestones

This section of Chapter 9 serves as a reminder in the whirlwind of a busy high-volume physical therapy clinic that taking a moment to celebrate achievements is essential for both personal and professional growth. In such a demanding environment, it's easy to get caught up in the daily routine, focusing solely on the next patient, the next appointment, or the next challenge. However, recognizing milestones and celebrating successes can be a game-changer in maintaining motivation and mental well-being.

The most rewarding milestones are the patient breakthroughs. These are the moments when you witness your patients making substantial progress or achieving their therapy goals. It might be the instant they experience a reduction in pain, regain mobility, or perform an exercise they couldn't do before. Celebrating these moments goes beyond just boosting their confidence; it reminds you of the meaningful impact you have on people's lives. Patient breakthroughs are a testament to the effectiveness of your care and provide a profound sense of fulfillment and pride in your work. Now... not to downplay the real focus here, which is absolutely the patient's achievement; however, it doesn't hurt here to ask your patient for a testimonial to showcase their success story, with their consent, on your clinic's website or social media. Also, set aside a budget for small trinkets, i.e. branded shades, t-shirts, sport bottles, head bands, neck gaiters, socks, beanies, etc that can be handed out as a reward and to encourage more milestones!

Acknowledging your professional milestones is equally important. These achievements can include completing a particularly challenging case, earning a certification, or mastering a new treatment technique. Every time you reach one of these milestones, it reflects your unwavering dedication and commitment to your craft. Professional growth ensures that you stay at the forefront of your field, continually improving your skills to provide the best care to your patients. As a reward for reaching a professional milestone, ask your clinic director or you splurge on yourself here and purchase a new piece of equipment or tool that can enhance your practice and make your job more efficient. Who doesn't love new toys!

In a busy clinic, you're part of a dynamic team, working together to provide top-notch care. Celebrating your team's achievements is vital, whether it's maintaining a consistently high level of patient satisfaction, hitting specific clinic goals, or developing innovative approaches to patient care. Team success reminds you that you're not alone in this demanding environment and encourages collaboration and cooperation among team members. Reward for team success is fun! Organize a team lunch or dinner to celebrate reaching clinic goals or maintaining high patient satisfaction rates. Plan a fun team-building event, like a weekend hike or an escape room challenge, to strengthen your bond as a clinic team. Keep a list of your colleagues' achievements with handwritten and then randomly handout thank-you notes, provide small tokens of appreciation, or include "shout-outs" during team meetings.

Never underestimate the importance of personal milestones. These could include achieving a fitness goal, maintaining a healthy work-life balance, or simply taking a well-deserved break to recharge. Your well-being is a critical factor in your ability to provide the best care, so celebrating your personal milestones is a form of self-care. The things that make you... you... are likely the same things that make you a great PT. When you achieve a personal milestone, dedicate a day for self-care, whether it's a spa day, hiking in nature, or enjoying a quiet day at home with your favorite book or movie. Remember, everyone loves toys, so purchase fitness-related equipment, like running shoes, a new yoga mat, or a fitness tracker to keep motivating yourself. Mentors are not just for professional growth, consider rewarding yourself by signing up for a mentorship program or engaging in professional coaching to foster your personal growth.

Positive affirmations

In the whirlwind of a busy clinic, it's easy to get caught up in the chaos. There are days when you might feel like you're running on autopilot, rushing from one patient to another, battling an ever-growing pile of paperwork, and barely catching a breath. This is where daily affirmations and recognizing small wins come in. They act as your anchors in the storm, reminding you why you chose this path and helping you maintain a positive mindset. I admit, giving yourself positive affirmations sounds cheesy (it did to me) but stay with me here, it really can help.

When you walk into your clinic, take a moment before you jump into the fray; say a positive affirmation. It could be as simple as "I am capable and confident in my abilities to help my patients today" or "I am resilient and adaptable in the face of challenges." Hell, even "I got this" can work. Repeat it to yourself, believe it, and let it set the tone for your day. In the clinic, it's common to second-guess yourself or feel overwhelmed. Affirmations counter these negative thoughts and replace them with positive ones. They reinforce your self-belief and help you stay focused on your goals. Affirmations can remind you that every day is an opportunity to learn and improve. They encourage a growth mindset, where challenges are seen as opportunities, and setbacks are stepping stones to success.

Celebrate the Small Wins

Make affirmations a part of your daily routine. Write them down, repeat them in the car on your way to work, or post them on your desk as visual reminders. Review it when you need a morale boost, especially on tough days. Encourage your colleagues with affirmations to them outloud. It fosters a positive team culture and provides mutual support. Affirmations are 100% effective, not even close and not every day will be a roaring success, and that's okay. It's all part of the journey. The only easy day was yesterday, so come back the next day ready to be better.

In a busy clinic, it's easy to forget the progress you make every day. Take a moment to acknowledge and celebrate even the smallest achievements. It could be helping a patient regain mobility or you finally conquering that pile of discharge charts or finishing a CEU course you've been putting off. Recognizing small wins boosts your motivation and keeps you engaged in your work. It reminds you that you're making a difference in your patients' lives, one step at a time. Celebrating wins, no matter how minor they seem, helps combat burnout. It's a reminder that your efforts are paying off, and you're on the right track. Consider rewarding your patients and yourself for these small wins. Pull out some of that clinic swag and toss it at patients when they check off a small win. Use the metacognition journal in the appendix or purchase the full journal at my website to reflect and motivate as you look back on what you have accomplished.

Seeking Feedback and Improvement

If you really want to grow professionally in a high-volume fast paced clinic, don't assume the answer is always in a book or in a course. Be daring and ask your patients what's working and what's not. Then, the hard part...listen to them. Their insights are gold and can help you fine-tune your approach. Their feedback helps you see beyond the symptoms and understand the impact of your care on their daily existence. It's a reality check that brings depth to your practice. Patient feedback isn't just a report card; it's your GPS guiding you through the therapy journey. It tells you if you're on the right path, need a slight detour, or should make a U-turn. It's your real-time course correction tool. When you actively seek and act on patient feedback, you're showing them that you value their perspective. This builds trust, fosters a strong therapeutic alliance, and increases their confidence in your abilities. Every patient is unique, and their feedback helps you learn and adapt. You'll discover what works and what doesn't, refine your skills, and grow as a therapist. It's like a continuous education program right in the clinic.

For patients, feedback is an opportunity to acknowledge their progress and efforts. When patients share positive feedback, it's a moment to celebrate their achievements, no matter how big or small. This feedback serves as recognition, making patients feel valued and motivated to keep working towards their goals. It becomes a source of encouragement for both patients and therapists, reinforcing that the hard work and collaboration are paying off.

For therapists, feedback is a form of validation. When patients provide positive feedback, it underscores the therapist's expertise and effectiveness, which is a significant professional success. Constructive feedback, on the other hand, helps therapists to celebrate progress in their skills and approach, highlighting areas for improvement and personal growth. Requesting feedback and practicing patient-centered care are achievements in themselves, as they reflect a commitment to the best possible care for patients.

Feedback can be as simple as open conversations during sessions, allowing patients to express their feelings and experiences. Additionally, using feedback forms or digital platforms, such as patient portals, can provide a structured way for patients to report their progress, pain levels, and overall experience. However, if you want to score social media bonus points for your clinic (which you should!), absolutely consider utilizing social media platforms like Google, Facebook, Twitter, Instagram, and LinkedIn. These platforms can help you stay connected with your patients and receive their feedback. You can regularly post content that showcases patient success stories, celebrating milestones in their rehabilitation journey. Additionally, you can run polls or surveys to directly collect feedback about the patient experience, clinic environment, and more. Integrating these tools into your clinic's social media strategy can keep your audience engaged, promote your services, and create a sense of community among your patients. I tend to use Google reviews for most of my patient feedback via social media. I incorporate Google Reviews into my daily practice by simply asking satisfied patients if they'd be willing to leave a review. If you choose this route, make sure your clinic's Google My Business profile is up to date and easily accessible so that patients can find it without hassle. I keep a QR code at the front desk and walk the patient over to the front desk. Positive reviews can be shared on your website or social media platforms, highlighting your clinic's achievements. Even negative reviews provide opportunities for growth and learning, which can be part of your feedback analysis.

When prompting feedback, keep the questions open-ended, like "How has your progress been?" or "Tell me more about how you're feeling." This invites patients to share their experiences. Patients should feel safe and comfortable sharing their thoughts. Be approachable, empathetic, and non-judgmental. When patients speak, listen attentively. Don't interrupt or rush through conversations. Let them express themselves fully. Patient feedback is gold, but it's worthless if you don't use it. If they mention discomfort, a particular exercise not working, or concerns about their treatment plan, take it seriously and make necessary adjustments. Patient feedback isn't a one-time deal. Continuously check in with them, assess their progress, and ask if there are any concerns or changes they'd like to see. If you receive positive feedback online, acknowledge the positive comments. If you receive negative reviews, don't get defensive! Acknowledge the feedback with appreciation for the opportunity to grow.

On the therapist's side, feedback tools and channels are equally essential. Regular meetings or discussions with colleagues can help in reflecting on individual practice and celebrating shared successes. Digital systems for tracking patient progress are valuable for analyzing trends and making data-driven decisions. Additionally, gathering peer feedback can provide a well-rounded perspective on personal performance. When collecting feedback, it's important to focus on specific aspects, such as the effectiveness of treatment techniques, patient satisfaction, and areas of improvement. Feedback should be incorporated into routine practice, influencing treatment decisions, and fostering an environment of continuous learning. Recognizing these achievements is essential for maintaining motivation and sustaining success in a busy clinic.

Inspiring Future Graduates

We stand on the shoulders of giants. In our profession, we each are the person standing on the shoulders. When you take the time to share your experiences and knowledge with aspiring physical therapy students, you become the giant, which not only benefits the student but also helps you thrive in a busy outpatient orthopedic clinic.

By talking to these future therapists, you can reflect on your own journey and offer valuable advice on how to handle the challenges of a high-volume clinic. This interaction may even lead to new insights that can help you improve your own practice. I went into writing this book with an idea of what I wanted to pass on to other PTs. Through the writing process, I have conducted a lot of professional and personal reflection followed by time organizing my thoughts. In real time, my focus on this book has helped sharpen my practice patterns.

Being the giant for these students can reignite your passion for your profession. Teaching can remind you why you became a physical therapist in the first place, which is motivating. It's a chance to assess your own career, reflect on your mission statement, set new goals, and keep growing as a therapist.

Taking on students in your clinic can be a two-way street. Students are often more connected to the latest research and developments because they are actively learning in the classroom. This means they can bring fresh insights, new techniques, and the most current evidence-based practices to your clinic. They might also help you keep pace with advancements in technology and treatments.

As these students gain updated knowledge, they can contribute to your clinic's professional development. Encouraging them to give in-services or presentations on recent research findings or emerging practices can be mutually beneficial. It can save you time researching and translating that information, and it empowers students to practice teaching, a skill they'll need as future therapists.

Balancing a busy patient schedule with the task of being an effective mentor isn't a walk in the park, but it's worth the effort. One way to do this is by setting aside specific times to work with your student, like short meetings during lunch breaks or before and after regular patient hours. To help you focus on mentorship, consider delegating administrative tasks to your support staff so you can concentrate on teaching.

Communication is crucial. Be clear about what you expect from your student and lay out the learning process upfront. This will ensure both of you know what you're working toward and can make the most of your time together. Create an environment where your student feels comfortable sharing thoughts and suggestions. Being open to their feedback can help tailor your mentorship style to better suit their needs.

Make good use of tools and resources. Digital platforms can be handy for sharing materials, giving feedback, or creating interactive lessons. Stress the importance of time management, staying organized, and staying current with the latest research. Mentorship can be streamlined by implementing templated curricula that guide both you and your student. You can find examples of 8- and 16-week curricula in the appendix that you can use or modify when taking on students.

Your Journey Begins

As we wrap up this insightful exploration of the bustling orthopedic PT clinic, take a moment to reflect on the transformative chapters that have shaped your narrative.

Welcome to the Clinic

The initial chaos and the steep learning curve have molded you into a resilient clinician. Embracing trials as learning opportunities, you've developed a keen instinct for navigating the unexpected turns and challenging moments that characterize clinic life.

Building Strong Foundations

Your commitment to patient-centered care has become your guiding principle. The journey through empathy and effective communication has not only established you as a trusted healthcare provider but has laid the foundation for lasting patient relationships.

Time Management and Scheduling

Juggling the demands of a high-volume clinic has become a finely tuned skill. Your expertise in scheduling strategies, coupled with efficient documentation and a prioritized focus on patient care, has transformed the chaotic schedule into a well-orchestrated routine.

Clinical Skills for Success

From the nuanced assessment of orthopedic conditions to crafting effective treatment plans, your clinical skills have evolved into a comprehensive toolkit. The artistry of employing manual therapy techniques and guiding patients toward discharge is a testament to your holistic approach.

Collaborative Care

The synergy within the clinic is a result of your efforts in nurturing interprofessional relationships. Clear communication with physicians and seamless teamwork have elevated patient care, creating an environment where collaboration is second nature.

Work-Life Balance

Finding equilibrium amidst the demands of the clinic, your journey in preventing burnout and embracing self-care has become an inspiration. Your ability to navigate the delicate balance between professional and personal life is a crucial aspect of your enduring success.

Patient Education and Empowerment

Guiding patients with realistic expectations and promoting compliance has been a pivotal aspect of your patient-centric approach. Your dedication to empowering patients for long-term health is a beacon of your commitment to their overall well-being.

Life-Long Learning and Standing On A Giant's Shoulders

Every day is a new chapter in your quest for knowledge and professional growth. Your dedication to continuous learning, networking, mentorship, and a well-thought-out career path has positioned you as a leader in the field.

Celebrate Your Successes

As you stand at the summit of achievements, remember to savor each victory. Recognizing milestones, embracing positive affirmations, seeking feedback, and inspiring future graduates reflect not just your personal triumphs but your contribution to the broader PT community.

In closing, your journey isn't just about surviving; it's about thriving, evolving, and leaving an enduring mark on the orthopedic physical therapy landscape. Cheers to the chaos, embracing the victories, and laying the foundation for a fulfilling, impactful career. Get after it!

10

APPENDIX

Empathy Statements

Empathy Statements

1. The following empathy statements are some examples I created from a continuing education I took that focused on patient communication. The statements have been modified from the original source to reflect a colloquial, relaxed voice. These are just examples, feel free to paraphrase in your own voice.
2. "I can tell you're hurting, but no worries, I'm here to help you deal with that pain."
3. "I totally get how frustrating it can be to deal with this injury. I'm your guide on the journey to recovery!"
4. "Your well-being is a big deal to me, and I've got your back every step of the way."
5. "Feeling a bit nervous? It's cool, we're in this together, and we'll make things better."
6. "I see this injury is cramping your style. Let's work together to get you back to your normal groove."
7. "You're putting in some serious effort, and it's really paying off. Keep it up!"
8. "Just want to say, I appreciate your hard work and dedication during your therapy sessions."
9. "If you've got any questions or concerns, don't be shy. I'm all ears."
10. "Pain? Everyone feels it differently. We'll tweak your treatment based on what works best for you."
11. "Your dedication is really showing, and I'm here to keep that momentum going."
12. "Your feedback is gold. It helps us fine-tune your therapy to meet your needs."

13. "I know you're facing some challenges, and we'll adjust our game plan to make it more doable for you. I want you to succeed."
14. "We all have good and bad days; I'm here to support you through all of them."
15. "Your determination is seriously impressive. I'm confident you'll keep rocking that progress."
16. "I'm here to create a comfy, safe space for your rehab journey."
17. "Injuries can be a real emotional rollercoaster too, and I'm here to help you through the ups and downs."
18. "Don't hold back – if you've got concerns or fears, let's tackle them together."
19. "I'm in it for the long haul, dedicated to helping you regain your strength and mobility."
20. "Your goals are my goals, and we'll work together to score those victories."
21. "I'm your support system, ready to provide the care and encouragement you need to get back to your awesome self!"
22. "Anyone would feel the same way in this situation, let's work on (fill in the blank): a solution / getting on track / a game plan together."

Smart Phrases

APPENDIX

Smart phrases

I suggest spending time upfront working on an identification system in your short cut abbreviations tool using a consistent prefix to identify the area of the SOAP note

I provided recommendations in the Subjective section below. My experience is that providers have their own preference for labeling these shortcuts. Find what works for you and go with it.

Initial Examination

Subjective:

1. "The patient reports a history of [relevant medical history]." SUBHX
2. "The patient's chief complaint is [chief complaint]." SUBCC
3. "Pain is localized to the [body part] and is described as [pain description]." SUBPAIN
4. "Pain level on a scale of 0-10 is [pain level] at rest and [pain level] during activity."SUBPNSCALE
5. "The patient reports a gradual onset of symptoms over [duration]." SUBONSET
6. "There is a history of [previous treatment] with limited improvement." SUBPRIORPT
7. "The patient notes [specific activities] exacerbate symptoms." SUBAGG
8. "No reports of numbness or tingling." SUBNNT
9. "Limited range of motion [joint]." SUBROM
10. "Patient denies any recent falls or trauma." SUBFALL

11. "No signs of radicular symptoms." SUBRAD
12. "No systemic symptoms reported." SUBNSS
13. "The patient has a past medical history of [relevant medical conditions]." SUBPMH
14. "The patient expresses concern about [specific functional limitation]." SUBPSFS

Activity Notes During Treatments:

1. "During today's session, the patient performed [specific exercises] with good form."
2. "Patient demonstrated improvement in [specific movement or technique]."
3. "Exercises were progressed to include [exercise progression]."
4. "Patient tolerated [modalities/treatments] well with no adverse reactions."
5. "Education provided on [specific home exercises/activities]."
6. "Patient demonstrated understanding of [body mechanics/ergonomics]."
7. "Compliance with home exercise program has been inconsistent."
8. "Patient exhibited improved mobility/flexibility in [specific area]."
9. "Manual therapy techniques were applied to [body part] with positive effect."
10. "Pain level during treatment was [pain level] and decreased to [pain level] post-treatment."
11. "Patient showed signs of increased confidence and de-

creased fear avoidance behaviors."
12. "Patient encouraged to maintain hydration and proper nutrition."
13. "Assisted patient with joint/muscle mobilization exercises."
14. "Reinforced proper body mechanics during [functional activity]."
15. "Instructed patient on pain management strategies, including [specific techniques]."

Goals:

1. "Short-term goal: Reduce pain to [pain level] during activities within [specific time frame]."
2. "Short-term goal: Improve range of motion by [degrees] within [specific time frame]."
3. "Short-term goal: Enhance strength in [muscle group] by [specific percentage] within [time frame]."
4. "Long-term goal: Restore functional independence for activities of daily living."
5. "Long-term goal: Improve balance and proprioception to reduce fall risk."
6. "Long-term goal: Increase patient's knowledge of condition and self-management techniques."
7. "Functional goal: Return to work with full duties by [specific date]."
8. "Functional goal: Resume recreational activities such as [specific activities] without pain."
9. "Goal: Reduce medication use for pain management within [time frame]."
10. "Goal: Achieve and maintain a body mass index (BMI) of

[specific value]."
11. "Educational goal: Instruct patient on signs of symptom exacerbation and when to seek medical attention."
12. "Social goal: Promote active participation in support groups and social activities."
13. "Goal: Improve sleep quality by implementing [specific sleep hygiene practices]."
14. "Goal: Enhance self-esteem and reduce anxiety associated with pain."
15. "Goal: Foster a positive patient-provider relationship through effective communication."

Assessment:

1. "The patient's condition is consistent with [diagnosis] based on clinical evaluation."
2. "Objective findings confirm [range of motion/strength] deficits."
3. "Pain assessment indicates [improvement/worsening/no change] since the previous visit."
4. "The patient demonstrates improved functional mobility in [specific tasks/activities]."
5. "Progress has been made toward achieving short-term goals."
6. "Patient's compliance with the home exercise program has improved."
7. "No adverse reactions to treatments or modalities observed."
8. "Objective measurements show a [percentage] increase in [specific parameter]."
9. "Patient's functional status has improved based on [spe-

cific functional assessment tool]."
10. "Patient exhibits a positive attitude and is motivated to achieve treatment goals."
11. "Education provided regarding [specific topic] has been well-received."
12. "Patient's pain management strategies have been effective in reducing symptoms."
13. "No signs of complications or red flags present."
14. "Recommend continuation of current plan of care with [frequency] visits."
15. "Scheduled follow-up evaluation in [specific time frame] to reassess progress."

Daily Note:

For daily notes, you can use similar smart phrases to the "Activity Notes During Treatments" section, focusing on the specific treatments and progress made during each session.

Progress Note:

For progress notes, use a combination of the smart phrases from the "Subjective," "Activity Notes During Treatments," and "Assessment" sections to summarize the patient's ongoing progress and any changes in their condition.

Discharge:

1. "Patient has met all short-term and long-term goals established during treatment."
2. "Functional independence has been restored, and the patient can perform [specific activities] without pain."

3. "Pain levels have decreased to a consistent [pain level] or less during activities."
4. "Patient exhibits good understanding of self-management techniques and is confident in managing their condition independently."
5. "Discharge recommendations include regular exercise and continued use of [specific self-management strategies]."
6. "Patient is advised to seek medical attention if there is a return of symptoms or worsening of condition."
7. "Follow-up visit with the primary care physician recommended for ongoing care."
8. "Discharge summary sent to the referring physician with detailed notes on the patient's progress and recommendations."
9. "Patient expressed satisfaction with treatment outcomes and understanding of the importance of ongoing self-care."
10. "No contraindications or precautions for discharge noted."
11. "The patient has embraced and successfully integrated ergonomic modifications into their work environment."
12. "Patient informed about community resources and support groups for continued well-being."
13. "The patient's overall health and well-being have improved significantly since the initial examination."
14. "The patient has demonstrated proper body mechanics and ergonomic principles applicable to their work environment."
15. "The patient's job-specific functional requirements have been assessed and met."

APPENDIX

Checklist for managing the urgency dilemma

Daily Checklist for Managing the Urgency Dilemma

Start your day by checking your schedule and categorizing patients:
  ☐ Post-op surgery
  ☐ Acute but not surgical
  ☐ Chronic pain (> 3 months) with fear avoidance/kinesiophobia
  ☐ Fall risk
  ☐ Routine daily visit
  ☐ Sports Performance

Urgency Slots: If part of your practice is to see urgent cases, try to set aside specific times for such cases and give your support team a heads-up.

Double-Booking Drama: Figure out which patients can handle double-booking (non-federal insurance peeps). Chat with your support crew to make sure they're down with it too.

Morning Huddle: Have a quick rounding with your support crew, exercise techs, and PTAs. Go through each patient's needs and what everyone's role is. Make sure it's all crystal clear.

Stay Loose: Be ready to shift gears as the day goes on. Sometimes, urgent cases pop
  up out of the blue, and you've got to roll with it.

Weekly Checklist for Managing the Urgency Dilemma:

Weekly Schedule Scan: Kick off the week by looking at your schedule. Ensure you've set aside enough time for different types of patients.

Urgency Slots All Week: Check that you've got spots for urgent cases spread out over the week. Make sure your support team knows the deal.

Double-Booking Prep: If you're thinking about double-booking for non-federal insurance patients, get your ducks in a row. Talk to your support team and make sure they're game.

Team Huddle: Hold a weekly team meeting to chat about upcoming patients and what they need. Remind everyone how teamwork and clear communication keep things flowing.

Stay Flexible: Encourage your support team to stay adaptable. Talk through different scenarios where you might need to switch up the schedule.

Balance Act: Review your weekly schedule to make sure you've got a good balance between urgent cases and patients with ongoing conditions.

Clinical Assessment Clusters for Common Orthopedic Conditions

APPENDIX

Clinical Assessment Clusters for Common Orthopedic Conditions

These are a few test cluster's or group of findings to keep in mind while performing an initial examination in a busy outpatient orthopedic clinic:

Cervical Spine Radiculopathy
- Positive Spurling's Test
- Positive Upper Limb Tension Test (ULTT)
- Dermatomal sensory changes and/or muscle weakness in the upper extremity
- Neck pain and radicular pain in a dermatomal pattern
- Cervical foraminal compression test

Cervical Spine Myelopathy
- Positive Hoffman's sign
- Hyperreflexia in upper limbs
- Clonus in upper limbs
- Gait disturbances and balance issues
- Positive Babinski sign

Shoulder Instability
- Positive Apprehension Test
- Positive Relocation Test
- History of recurrent shoulder dislocations
- Generalized ligamentous laxity
- Positive Sulcus Sign
- Positive Load and Shift Test (Labrum)
- Pain with overhead and throwing activities (Labrum)

☐Positive O'Brien's Test (Labrum)

Rotator Cuff Tear (Full and Partial Thickness)
☐Positive Jobe's Test (Empty Can Test)
☐Pain and weakness with resisted abduction
☐Positive Drop Arm Test
☐Pain and weakness with resisted external rotation
☐Positive Hawkins-Kennedy Test

Shoulder Impingement
☐Positive Neer's Test
☐Positive Hawkin's Test
☐Pain with overhead activities
☐Limited range of motion, especially in abduction and external rotation
☐Weakness in the supraspinatus muscle

Shoulder Adhesive Capsulitis (Frozen Shoulder)
☐Limited active and passive range of motion, (in particular ER at side < 30 deg)
☐Pain and stiffness in the shoulder, especially at night
☐Gradual onset of symptoms
☐Positive Codman's Drop Arm Test
☐Positive Hawkins-Kennedy Test

Thoracic Outlet Syndrome
☐Positive Adson's Test
☐Positive Wright's Test
☐Numbness and tingling in the upper extremity
☐Symptoms worsen with arm elevation
☐Positive Roos Test (Elevated Arm Stress Test)

APPENDIX

Lumbar Spine Radiculopathy
- Positive Straight Leg Raise Test (SLR)
- Dermatomal sensory changes and/or muscle weakness in the lower extremity
- Pain radiating down the leg
- Positive Crossed Straight Leg Raise Test
- Positive Bragard's Test

Cauda Equina Syndrome
- Saddle anesthesia (loss of sensation in the perianal area)
- Urinary Retention
- Fecal incontinence
- Severe low back pain
- Bilateral leg weakness or paralysis

Lumbar Spine Stenosis
- Neurogenic claudication (pain and cramping with walking)
- Relief of symptoms with lumbar flexion (e.g., sitting down)
- Positive Slump Test
- Pain radiating into the buttocks and legs
- Reduced lumbar range of motion

Hip Labral Tear
- Positive FABER (Patrick's) Test
- Groin pain
- Clicking or catching in the hip
- Positive anterior impingement test
- Limited hip range of motion

Hip Osteoarthritis
- Reduced hip range of motion

- Groin and/or lateral hip pain
- Morning stiffness
- Pain with weight-bearing activities
- Positive Trendelenburg Test

Patellar Tendinopathy vs. Patellofemoral Pain Syndrome
- Tenderness at the inferior patellar pole (Tendinopathy)
- Pain with resisted knee extension (Tendinopathy)
- Positive Jumper's Knee Test (Patellar Tendinopathy)
- Anterior knee pain with activities like stairs and squatting (Patellofemoral Pain Syndrome)
- Positive Clarke's Sign (Patellofemoral Pain Syndrome)

Tibialis Posterior Tendon Dysfunction
- Posterior tibial tendon pain and swelling
- Pain and difficulty with single-leg heel raise
- Pes planus (flat foot deformity)
- Positive Talar Tilt Test
- Positive Navicular Drop Test

Ankle Sprain vs. Fracture
- Swelling and bruising around the ankle (both)
- Tenderness at the medial and lateral malleoli (both)
- Inability to bear weight (fracture)
- Positive Ottawa Ankle Rules (to rule out fracture)
- Positive Anterior Drawer Test (sprain)

These clusters of findings can help speed up your initial assessment and differential diagnosis for patients with various orthopedic conditions. It's essential to combine clinical tests with patient history, symptom presentation, and imaging when necessary to arrive at an accurate diagnosis and treatment plan. Also, this list is not exhaustive. These are just some very common cases that often walk through the clinic door.

Treatment Based Classification System

APPENDIX

Treatment Based Classification

Lumbar Spine

1. *Manipulation/Mobilization*
   a. Lumbar Strain / sprain
      i. + CPR
         1. Symptoms < 16 days since onset
         2. No radicular symptoms
         3. Hypomobility of at least 1 vertebrae with segmental testing
         4. At least 1 hip demonstrates Internal Rotation > 35 deg
      ii. Trigger points appreciated within the lumbar paraspinal muscles
   b. Facet impingement
      i. + closing pattern (symptoms with extension and ipsilateral side bending)
   c. Sacroiliac Joint Dysfunction
      i. + Sacroiliac Joint Dysfunction Cluster (Laslett's Cluster)
         1. (+ thigh thrust / + compression / + distraction / + Gaenslen's / + sacral compression)
      ii. + Fortin finger point over SIJ
      iii. + Groin pain

2. *Direction Specific / Exercise Specific Group*
   a. Extension Responder (symptoms improve with extension)
      i. Disc bulge / herniation
         1. Active/Passive Straight Leg Raise (SLR)
         2. + L5 myotomal weakness
         3. + Crossed SLR
         4. + Slump Test
   b. Flexion Responder (symptoms improve with flexion)
      i. Lumbar spine spondylosis stenosis (central stenosis / lateral foraminal / both)
      ii. Lumbar spine spondylolysis
      iii. Lumbar spondylolisthesis

3. *Stabilization:*
   a. Lumbar segmental instability
      i. Returns from forward bend with aberrant movement (Gower)
      ii. < 40 years old
      iii. Active SLR > 90
      iv. + Prone instability test
      v. +6/9 Beighton Score
   b. Congenital hypermobility
      i. Increased painful arc with low back flexion
      ii. Gower's sign

4. *Nociplastic*
   a. Kinesiophobia / Central pain sensitization
      i. + pain > 3 months (Chronic pain)
      ii. + hypersensitivity (Allodynia)
      iii. ODI > 50% (work related fears/satisfaction)
      iv. Orebro > 105

SURVIVE AND THRIVE

Treatment Based Classification

Cervical spine TBCS

1. ***Neck pain with Mobility Deficits***

   a. Cervical spondylosis
   b. Facet syndrome
   c. Mechanical neck pain (strain/sprain) / WAD

2. ***Neck Pain with Radiating Pain***

   a. Spurling A
   b. Cervical spine distraction eases symptoms
   c. Active ROM rotation < 60 deg to the affected side
   d. Upper Limb Tension Test A
   e. (+) arm squeeze

3. ***Neck Pain with Movement Coordination Deficit***

   a. Deep Neck Flexor muscle endurance < 39 seconds for males and 29 seconds for females
   b. Aberrant neck movements with active ROM (most common when going into or coming out of extension)
   c. Trigger points appreciated within cervical paraspinal muscles/soft tissue
   d. Mid-range neck pain that increases at end range

4. ***Neck Pain with Headaches***

   a. Limited mobility in OA/AA (C0-C1 and C2-C2, respectively)
   b. Headaches with segmental testing
   c. Limited Active ROM in all directions but mostly in extension or rotation to the effected side
   d. Cervical and Thoracic segmental hypomobility
   e. (+) Deep Neck Flexor Endurance Test

APPENDIX

CASE STUDY #1
Combining Test Clusters, SFMA and TBCS

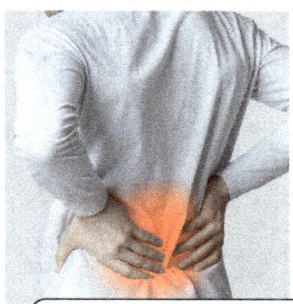

Name: John Doe
Age: 42 years old
Occupation: Office worker

John Doe presented with complaints of chronic low back pain, which he reported experiencing for the past six months. He described the pain as a dull ache that was primarily located in the lower back. Patient reports pain mostly across his low back that occasionally travels into his buttock area on both sides but doesn't recall symptoms going down his thigh or below his knee. He mentioned that the pain intensity increases with prolonged sitting and is partially relieved when he lays on his stomach or stands. There was no reported trauma or specific incident that initiated the pain.

Imaging: none at this time

Physical Examination

Quick Nerve and Special Test Screening:
Straight Leg Raise Test (-) bilaterally.
Slump Test: (-) bilaterally
Reflexes: All deep tendon reflexes (patellar and Achilles) WNL
Sensory Testing: Unremarkable

Postural Assessment: The patient presented with an increased lumbar lordosis.

SFMA: Cervical Flexion
1. A/PROM Dysfunctional, Non-painful
2. Upper cervical spine flexion (C0-C1 Mobility Dysfunction)

Cervical Spine Extension
1. Functional, Non-painful

Cervical Spine Rotation
1. Dysfunctional, Non-painful bilaterally
2. Thoracic rotation Mobility Dysfunction

Multisegmental Spine Flexion
1. Dysfunctional, painful
2. A/PSLR dysfunctional = Posterior thigh tissue extensibility dysfunction

Multisegmental Spine Extension
1. Dysfunctional, painful
2. Cobra position with 2 AirEx pads Functional, Non-painful = Mobility Dysfunction
3. + Thomas Test bilateral (Anterior hip mobility dysfunction)
4. FABER (-)

Multisegmental Spine Rotation
1. Dysfunctional, Non-painful bilaterally
2. Thoracic rotation Mobility Dysfunction

UE Pattern 1 (Reaching Up the Back)
1. Functional, Non-painful

UE Pattern 2 (Reaching Down the Back)
1. Dysfunctional, Non-painful bilateral
2. Shoulder Flexion Tissue Extensibility Dysfunction (Latissimus Doris)

Single Leg Balance
1. Eyes Open Functional, Non-painful
2. Eyes Closed Dysfunctional, Non-painful bilateral = Proprioception Dysfunction

Arms-Down Squat
1. Dysfunctional, Non-painful
2. Unable to squat below 90 degrees
3. Half kneeling ankle DF 15 deg bilateral = mobility dysfunction

CASE STUDY #1
Combining Test Clusters, SFMA and TBCS

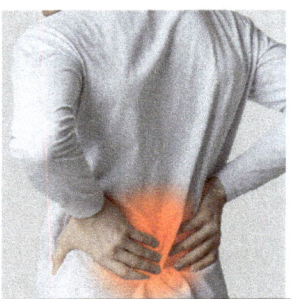

Palpation: Tenderness and muscle spasm noted in the lumbar paraspinals

Accessory Motion: Posterior to Anterior stiffness with pain appreciated at L3/4 and L4/5

Treatment Based Classification = Manipulation/Mobilization
1. Lumbar Strain / sprain
    a. + CPR
        i. < 16d (-)
        ii. no radicular sx (+)
        iii. Hypomobility (+)
        iv. hip IR > 35 deg (-)
    b. Trigger points (+)
2. Stabilization:
    a. Lumbar segmental instability
        i. aberrant movement (Gower)
        ii. < 40 yoa
        iii. SLR > 90
        iv. + PIT

The patient's presentation, including a history of chronic low back pain, and positive SFMA findings, John Doe was classified into the Manipulation/Mobilization Group. Note that spinal manipulation in this case may not be effective due to chronicity of John's symptoms. Rather, John would likely benefit from joint and tissue mobilization. The SFMA provided some key areas to target, such as Thoracic spine rotation mobility, posterior thigh tissue extensibility, ankle dorsiflexion mobility, anterior hip lengthening and anterior trunk muscle performance. This patient would also benefit from patient education related to workspace ergonomics and participating in a regular routine of aerobic exercise. The following is an example of a 6-week progression for Mr. Doe.

The following is an example of a 6-week progression for Mr. Doe.

APPENDIX

CASE STUDY 1: WEEKS 1-2

CLINIC DAYS

Energy System Development
1. Recumbent bike or Elliptical x 6 minutes

Education:
1. Ergonomic adjustments for her workstation.
2. Techniques for maintaining good posture.
3. Pain management strategies, including activity modification.

Manual Therapy
1. ASTYM if credentialed
2. Trigger point release via IASTM, Dry needling or cupping
3. Foam Roll T-spine, TFL-ITB

Activation Exercises
1. Dynamic warm-up
2. Cat camel / Half kneeling hip flexor / thread the needle / Brettzel 1.0 / bird dog
3. Ankle flips / Knee to chest walk / Punter walk
4. SFMA Correctives
5. Glute activation: Monster walk matrix / glute bridge / resisted clamshell

Functional Circuit 1
1. Wall sit
2. Wall plank
3. Paloff press

Functional Circuit 2
1. HK MB chops/lifts
2. Hip hinge training
3. Farmer walk

HOME EXERCISE

Dynamic Warm-Up
1. Cat camel / Half kneeling hip flexor / thread the needle / Brettzel 1.0 / bird dog

Activation Exercises
1. Glute Activation: Monster walk matrix / glute bridge / resisted clamshell

Functional Circuit 1
1. Wall push-ups
2. Wall sit
3. SL balance with isometric hip abduction

Functional Circuit 2
1. Elevated shoulder taps
2. 1-arm band row
3. Hip hinges

CASE STUDY 1: WEEKS 3-4

CLINIC DAYS

Energy System Development
1. Recumbent bike or Elliptical x 6 minutes

Manual Therapy
1. ASTYM if credentialed
2. Trigger point release via IASTM, Dry needling or cupping
3. Foam Roll T-spine, TFL-ITB, Hamstrings, QL

Activation Exercises
1. Dynamic warm-up
2. Cat camel / child's pose thread the needle / Brettzel 1.0 / bird dog holds
3. SFMA Correctives
4. Punter walk / Lunge Twist / Forward T
5. Glute activation: Monster walk matrix / band squat / band fire hydrant

Functional Circuit 1
1. Goblets squats
2. Floor plank
3. Paloff press walk out

Functional Circuit 2
1. Standing MB chops/lifts
2. DB Deadlifts
3. 1-arm low Farmer walk

HOME EXERCISE

Dynamic Warm-Up
1. Cat camel / Half kneeling hip flexor / thread the needle / Brettzel 1.0 / bird dog

Activation Exercises
1. Glute Activation: Monster walk matrix / glute bridge / resisted clamshell

Functional Circuit 1
1. Primal push ups
2. Squats
3. Modified side plank with leg lift

Functional Circuit 2
1. Elevated shoulder taps
2. Quadruped DB row
3. Dead bug

CASE STUDY 1: WEEKS 5-6

CLINIC DAYS

Energy System Development
1. Elliptical or Treadmill x 6 minutes

Manual Therapy
1. ASTYM if credentialed
2. Trigger point release via IASTM, Dry needling or cupping
3. Foam Roll T-spine, TFL-ITB, Hamstrings, QL

Activation Exercises
1. Dynamic warm-up
2. Cat camel / child's pose thread the needle / Brettzel 1.0 / bird dog holds
3. SFMA Correctives
4. Knee to Chest + Lunge Twist / Forward T + Punter walk
5. Glute activation: Monster walk matrix / 1-leg bridge / standing clamshell

Functional Circuit 1
1. Split squats
2. ¼ TGU
3. Quadruped DB drag

Functional Circuit 2
1. 1-leg Deadlifts
2. High/Low Farmer walk
3. DB renegade row

HOME EXERCISE

Dynamic Warm-Up
1. Cat camel / Half kneeling hip flexor / thread the needle / Brettzel 1.0 / bird dog

Activation Exercises
1. Glute Activation: Monster walk matrix / band squats / glute bridge / band clamshell / band donkey kick

Functional Circuit 1
1. Beast crawl
2. Split Squats
3. Copenhagen plank

Functional Circuit 2
1. Push ups
2. Hip hinge + DB row
3. 90/90 LTRs

CASE STUDY #2
Combining Test Clusters, SFMA and TBCS

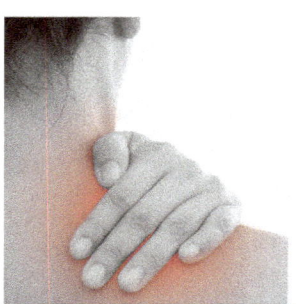

Name: Mrs. Johnson
Age: 52 years old
Occupation: HR Manager

Mrs. Johnson seeks assistance for persistent neck discomfort that has been bothering her for the past six months. She mentions that the pain often starts at the base of her neck and radiates towards the shoulders. Mrs. Johnson attributes it to the long hours she spends typing and staring at the computer screen. She denies any recent trauma or injury to the neck.

History:
- Gradual onset of neck discomfort
- Radiating pain towards the shoulders but does not reports symptom below shoulders
- Aggravated by prolonged computer work
- No history of recent trauma

Physical Examination:

TBCS/SFMA Findings: Cervical Flexion
1. Supine AROM Dysfunctional, non-painful
2. Supine PROM Functional, non-painful

Cervical Spine Extension
1. AROM Functional, non-painful (no radicular symptoms)

Cervical Spine Rotation
1. A/PROM rotation dysfunctional, non-painful bilateral but > 60 degrees without radicular pain
2. C1-2 ROM WNL

UE Pattern 1
1. AROM Functional, Non-painful

UE Pattern 2
1. AROM Dysfunctional, Painful
2. Prone PROM Functional, Non-painful

Special Tests:
1. ULTT A: Negative
2. Deep Neck Flexor Endurance: 15 seconds

Palpation:
1. Tenderness to palpation and trigger points appreciated throughout bilateral upper trapezius, levator scapula, and rhomboids

Mrs. Johsnon demonstrates signs and symptoms consistent with the Treatment-based Classification System (TBCS) of Neck Pain with Movement Coordination Deficit. Additionally, The SFMA findings demonstrate several areas of stability and motor control dysfunction. The following is an example of a 6-week progression for Mrs. Johnson.

The following is an example of a 6-week progression for Mrs. Johnson.

APPENDIX

CASE STUDY 2: WEEKS 1-2

CLINIC DAYS

Energy System Development
1. UBE x 6 minutes

Education
1. Ergonomic adjustments for her workstation.
2. Techniques for maintaining good posture.
3. Pain management strategies, including activity modification.

Manual Therapy
- ASTYM
- Trigger point release via IASTM, Dry needling or cupping
- Foam Roll T-spine and shoulder matrix

Activation Exercises
- Dynamic warm-up
- Cat camel / bird dog / thread the needle / Brettzel 2.0
- SFMA Correctives
- Rotator Cuff Activation: External rotation with resistance band
- Isometric Neck Holds: 4-way band resisted walk out

Functional Circuit 1:
- Supine arm bar rolls
- Quadruped shoulder closed-kinetic chain matrix
- Half kneeling band rows

Functional Circuit 2:
- Supine band isometric diagonal holds with head nods, rotations
- Quadruped horizontal abduction reach with head rotations
- Farmer walks

HOME EXERCISE

Dynamic Warm-Up
1. Neck stretches
2. Shoulder rolls
3. Cat-Cow stretches

Activation Exercises
1. Rotator Cuff Activation: Side-lying external rotations
2. Deep Neck Flexor Activation: Supine chin tucks

Functional Circuit 1
1. Neck isometrics against a pillow
2. Wall push-ups
3. Wall angels

Functional Circuit 2
1. and arm lift
2. Beginner bird dog
3. Supine LTRs with emphasis on scapular stabilization

CASE STUDY 2: WEEKS 3-4

CLINIC DAYS

Energy System Development
1. UBE x 6 minutes

Manual Therapy
1. ASTYM
2. Trigger point release via IASTM, Dry needling or cupping
3. Foam Roll T-spine and shoulder matrix

Activation Exercises
1. Dynamic warm-up
2. Cat camel / bird dog / thread the needle / Brettzel 2.0
3. SFMA Correctives
4. Punter walk / Lunge Twist / Forward T
5. Rotator Cuff Activation: Shoulder OKC matrix
6. Isometric Neck Holds: Quadruped band resisted neck retraction

Functional Circuit 1
1. Half kneeling windmill
2. DB shoulder matrix
3. Standing band row matrix

Functional Circuit 2
1. HK Band D1/D2 hold with head rotations/nods
2. Shoulder taps
3. Mid-carry farmer walks

HOME EXERCISE

Dynamic Warm-Up
1. Cat camel / bird dog / thread the needle / Brettzel 2.0
2. SFMA Correctives

Activation Exercises
1. Rotator Cuff Activation: standing 90/90 external rotation
2. Deep Neck Flexor Activation: Supine chin tucks + crunch

Functional Circuit 1
1. Prone and side plank variations
2. DB scaption
3. Bent over DB Row

Functional Circuit 2
1. Bent over Scarecrow to OH reach
2. 1-arm counter top serratus press
3. Dead bug

APPENDIX

CASE STUDY 2: WEEKS 5-6

CLINIC DAYS

Energy System Development
1. UBE x 6 minutes

Manual Therapy
1. ASTYM
2. Trigger point release via IASTM, Dry needling or cupping
3. Foam Roll T-spine and shoulder matrix

Activation Exercises
1. Dynamic warm-up
2. Cat camel / bird dog / thread the needle / Brettzel 2.0
3. SFMA Correctives
4. Punter walk to Forward T
5. Knee to Chest to Lunge Twist
6. Rotator Cuff Activation: Shoulder OKC matrix
7. Deep neck flexor Activation: High plank band resisted neck retraction

Functional Circuit 1
1. ¼ Turkish Get Up
2. HK band chops and lifts
3. Bird Dog DB Row

Functional Circuit 2
1. Push-up progression
2. Face Pulls
3. Overhead farmer walks

HOME EXERCISE

Dynamic Warm-Up
1. Cat camel / bird dog / thread the needle / Brettzel 2.0
2. SFMA Correctives

Activation Exercises
1. Rotator Cuff Activation: Bento over ITYW
2. Deep Neck Flexor Activation: Quadruped

Functional Circuit 1
1. Prone plank with reaches
2. DB Arnold Press
3. High plank DB Row to T-plank

Functional Circuit 2
1. Wall 1-arm band push ups
2. Dead bug with pull over
3. Straight leg LTR with band pull apart

Recommended Reading

APPENDIX

Recommended Reading

Leadership and Management

1. Leaders Eat Last (Sinek)
2. Drive: The Surprising Truth About What Motivates Us (Pink)
3. The 5 Levels of Leadership (Maxwell)
4. Emotional Intelligence (Goleman)
5. Good to Great (Collins)
6. Extreme Ownership (Willink and Babin)
7. Dichotomy of Leadership (Willink and Babin)
8. Leadership Strategies and Tactics (Willink)
9. Discipline Equals Freedom (Willink)
10. The Responsible Company (Chouinard)

Healthcare Administration

1. Who Moved My Cheese (Johnson)
2. The Innovator's Prescription (Christensen)
3. If Disney Ran Your Hospital (Lee)
4. Switch (Heath)
5. Influencer: The Power to Change Anything (Patterson)

Communication and Team Building

1. Crucial Conversations (Patterson)
2. Team of Teams: New Rules of Engagement for a Complex

World (McChrystal)
3. Dare to Lead: Brave Work. Tough Conversations. Whole Hearts (Brown)
4. Influence: Psychology of Persuasion (Cialdini)
5. Motivational Interviewing (Miller)

Personal Development

1. 7 Habits of Highly Successful People (Covey)
2. Atomic Habits (Clear)
3. 21 Suggestions for Success (Brown)
4. Power of Willpower (Taylor)
5. Willpower, Rediscovering The Greatest Human Strength (Baumeister)
6. High Performance Habits (Burchard)
7. The Habit Factor (Grunberg)
8. The Obstacle is The Way (Holiday)
9. The Motivation Manifesto (Burchard)
10. The Miracle Morning (Elrod)
11. The Year of Magical Thinking (Didion)
12. Thinking Big (Tracy)
13. Power of Positive Thinking (Peale)
14. What Should I Do With My Life (Bronson)
15. Man's Search for Meaning (Franki)
16. How Good People Make Tough Choices (Kidder)
17. Essentialism (McKeown)
18. The Power of Less (Babauta)
19. Slight Edge (Olson)
20. Can't Hurt Me (Goggins)

Philosophy and Well-Being

1. Tao Te Ching (Tzu)
2. Sapiens (Harari)
3. Homo Deus (Harari)
4. 21 Lessons for the 21st Century (Harari)

Health and Wellness

1. Flow (Csikszentmihalyi)
2. Breath: New Science of a Lost Art (Nestor)
3. Deep (Nestor)
4. Get High Now (without drugs) (Nestor)

Physical Therapy and Movement Science

1. Movement (Cook)
2. Business of Movement (Cook)
3. Bridging the Gap (Falsone)
4. Running Rewired (Dicharry)
5. Run Like an Athlete (Dicharry)
6. Ready to Run (Starrett)
7. Deskbound (Starrett)
8. Becoming a Supple Leopard (Starrett)
9. New Functional Training in Sport (Boyle)
10. Advances in Functional Training (Boyle)
11. Before We Go (Dan John)
12. Can You Go (Dan John)
13. Never Let Go (Dan John)

14. No What? (Dan John)

Certifications / Specializations

Certifications / Specializations

Orthopedic Clinical Specialist (OCS): A certification indicating advanced knowledge, experience, and skills in orthopedics.

Sports Clinical Specialist (SCS): Focuses on acute and chronic sports injuries and rehabilitation.

Certified Strength and Conditioning Specialist (CSCS): Offered by the National Strength and Conditioning Association (NSCA), it focuses on strength and conditioning training for athletes.

Certified Athletic Trainer (ATC): While primarily for athletic trainers, this certification can be beneficial for physical therapists working in sports rehab.

Certified Manual Physical Therapist (CMPT): This certification involves specialized training in manual therapy techniques.

Certified Orthopedic Manual Therapist (COMT): Focuses on advanced manual therapy skills for orthopedic conditions.

Functional Movement Systems (FMS): Certification in assessing and improving movement patterns for injury prevention and performance enhancement.

Selective Functional Movement Assessment (SFMA): A series of full-body movement tests designed to assess fundamental patterns of movement in patients with known musculoskeletal pain.

Certification in Applied Functional Science (CAFS): Focuses on functional assessment and treatment strategies.

Certification in Mechanical Diagnosis and Therapy (MDT): Also known as the McKenzie Method, focuses on the assessment and treatment of spinal and extremity musculoskeletal disorders.

Movement System Impairment (MSI) Certification: emphasizes the identification and correction of inefficient muscle activation patterns, joint movement limitations, and improper biomechanics during movement to treat and prevent musculoskeletal pain and dysfunction.

Certified Exercise Expert for Aging Adults (CEEAA): Useful for therapists working with older adults in an outpatient setting.

American Board of Physical Therapy Specialties (ABPTS) certifications: Apart from OCS and SCS, they offer other specialty areas that might be relevant depending on the therapist's interest.

Performance Enhancement Specialist (PES): Offered by the National Academy of Sports Medicine (NASM), focusing on improving athletic performance.

Corrective Exercise Specialist (CES): Another NASM certification, focusing on corrective exercise strategies.

Dry Needling Certification: For therapists who want to use dry needling in their practice.

ASTYM Certification: teaches PT's how to regenerate healthy soft tissues (muscles, tendons, etc.) and eliminate or reduce unwanted scar tissue using specialized tools to deliver treatment

Blood Flow Restriction Training Certification: Specialized training technique used for strength and conditioning, as well as rehabilitation.

Aquatic Therapy Certification: For therapists using aquatic therapy in orthopedic and sports rehab.

Pilates Certification for Rehabilitation: Using Pilates techniques in rehabilitation settings.

Kinesio Taping Certification: Specialized training in the use of kinesio tape for therapeutic purposes.

Board Certified Sports Dietitian (CSSD): Relevant for integrating nutrition into sports rehab and conditioning.

This list is definitely not exhaustive but it's a good start to knowing what certifications and specializations are out there.

Templates for Clinical Mentorship

APPENDIX

Templates for Clinical Mentorship

<u>For an 8-week clinic affiliation, here's an example:</u>

Week 1-2: Introduction

- Clinic orientation
- Introduction to electronic medical records
- Shadowing sessions
- Discuss and set initial learning objectives

Week 3-4: Clinical Skills

- Basic assessment techniques
- Exposure to common conditions
- Basic treatment techniques
- Observation and guided practice

Week 5-6: Application of Skills

- Direct involvement with patients
- Patient interaction and communication
- Creating exercise programs
- Assisting in documentation

Week 7-8: Integration

- Advanced skills in assessments
- Hands-on treatment techniques
- Developing clinical reasoning
- Gradual increase in independence

For a 16-week affiliation, continue with the following:

Week 9-10: Specialized Areas

- Exposure to niche areas like sports therapy or geriatrics
- Hands-on experience and role-specific skills

Week 11-12: Advanced Clinical Reasoning

- Advanced case studies
- Complex patient profiles
- Treatment planning and decision-making

Week 13-14: Interdisciplinary Exposure

- Collaboration with other healthcare providers
- Interdisciplinary rounds and meetings
- Understanding the role of PT in a holistic healthcare approach

Week 15-16: Reflecting and Future Planning

- Self-assessment and goal setting
- Preparing for board exams or future career prospects
- Reflecting on the entire clinical experience

APPENDIX

CELEBRATING SMALL WINS

Date:

1. What was a professional achievement or success you experienced today?

2. Share a specific professional accomplishment or positive outcome

3. What personal accomplishment or positive experience brightened your day?

4. Describe a moment when you felt personally fulfilled or content.

5. Highlight a patient's progress or a success story that made your day.

6. Reflect on any events, lessons, or growth moments from your day.

SURVIVE AND THRIVE

GRATITUDE

TAKE A MOMENT TO REFLECT

DATE

LIST THREE THINGS OR PEOPLE YOU'RE GRATEFUL FOR TODAY.

LIST ANY CHALLENGES FROM THE DAY

LIST THREE GOALS FOR TOMORROW

1

2

3

PLAN FOR WHAT YOU WANT TO ACCOMPLISH AND FOCUS ON TOMORROW.

SOMETHING THAT INSPIRED ME TODAY

TODAYS SELF-CARE

NOTES & FREE THOUGHTS

APPENDIX

METACOGNITION DAILY ENTRY PAGE

01 MORNING REFLECTION • WHAT DRIVES YOU IN YOUR CAREER?

02 PRIORITIZE GOALS • SPECIFY YOUR CAREER GOALS AND ASPIRATIONS

03 THOUGHTS & FEELINGS • IDENTIFY YOUR CORE VALUES, E.G., PATIENT-CENTERED CARE, EVIDENCE-BASED PRACTICE, COMPASSION

04 END OF DAY REFLECTION • LIST YOUR CURRENT SKILLS AND ABILITIES

05 SUCCESSES • IDENTIFY AREAS FOR IMPROVEMENT

METACOGNITION DAILY ENTRY PAGE

06 AREAS OF IMPROVEMENT • WHAT DRIVES YOU IN YOUR CAREER?

07 LEARNING MOMENTS • SPECIFY YOUR CAREER GOALS AND ASPIRATIONS

08 LOOKING AHEAD: PRIORITIES AND GOALS

• IDENTIFY YOUR CORE VALUES, E.G., PATIENT-CENTERED CARE, EVIDENCE-BASED PRACTICE, COMPASSION

CREATING YOUR MISSION STATEMENT

01 MY PURPOSE • WHAT DRIVES YOU IN YOUR CAREER?

_____

02 MY GOALS • SPECIFY YOUR CAREER GOALS AND ASPIRATIONS

_____

03 MY VALUES • IDENTIFY YOUR CORE VALUES, E.G., PATIENT-CENTERED CARE, EVIDENCE-BASED PRACTICE, COMPASSION

_____

04 MY SKILLS & ABILITIES • LIST YOUR CURRENT SKILLS AND ABILITIES

_____

05 SKILLS & ABILITIES TO DEVELOP • IDENTIFY AREAS FOR IMPROVEMENT

_____

06 KNOWLEDGE TRACKS • MENTION THE KNOWLEDGE AREAS YOU WANT TO FOCUS ON

_____

07 IMPACT • DESCRIBE THE IMPACT YOU WANT TO HAVE ON PATIENTS, THE PROFESSION, AND HEALTHCARE

_____

About the Author

Adam Reece is a seasoned Physical Therapist with a broad expertise in the area of orthopedics. Recognized as a Doctor of Physical Therapy and a board-certified orthopedic specialist (OCS), Adam is at the forefront of patient care and clinician leadership.

Based in Everett, WA, Adam currently serves as the Lead Physical Therapist in a high-volume outpatient orthopedic and sports clinic. His role demands not only clinical proficiency but also a deep understanding of the dynamics that define a busy orthopedic setting. Adam thrives in the organized chaos, transforming challenges into opportunities for growth.

Before embarking on his journey in physical therapy, Adam was the civilian fitness program manager with the U.S. Navy MWR Fitness Enhancement Program in San Diego, CA. This early experience laid the groundwork for his passion for movement, health, and the holistic well-being of individuals.

Adam's commitment to continuous learning and professional development is evident not only in his extensive clinical acumen but also in his role as a mentor and educator. His insights into surviving and thriving in a high-volume outpatient orthopedic clinic are distilled from years of hands-on experience and a dedication to elevating patient care.

Beyond the clinic, Adam is a dynamic individual who embraces the challenges of the profession with enthusiasm. His unique journey, from military fitness leadership to becoming a respected figure in orthopedic physical therapy, offers readers a genuine perspective on the demands and rewards of the field.

As you delve into the pages of this book, know that the wisdom shared is not just theoretical—it's a reflection of Adam's day-to-day reality as a leader, practitioner, and advocate for excellence in orthopedic care.

Adam Reece, DPT, OCS
Copyright 12/2023

🌐 **Deltaperformancerehab.com**

www.ingramcontent.com/pod-product-compliance
Lightning Source LLC
Chambersburg PA
CBHW071208240526
45470CB00018B/1637